MW00399485

MEZCAL
and
TEQUILA
COCKTAILS

EMANUELE MENSAH

WHALEN
BOOK · WORKS

Kennebunkport, Maine

Books published by Whalen Book Works are available at special discounts when purchased in bulk. For more information, please email us at info@whalenbookworks.com.

Whalen Book Works
68 North Street
Kennebunkport, ME 04046

www.whalenbookworks.com

Cover and interior design by Melissa Gerber
Photography by Emanuele Mensah
Images on pages 4, 83, 101, 135, and 175
used under official license from Shutterstock.com.
Typography: Gotham, Adobe Caslon, and Eveleth Clean Thin

Printed in China
1 2 3 4 5 6 7 8 9 0

First Edition

"Tootoote tootoote, yerenom nsa na yerefa adwen."

*Translated from Twi (Ghanian): Little by little,
little by little, while we are drinking we make plans.*

CONTENTS

INTRODUCTION

El elíxir de los dioses (the elixir of the gods)

When someone asks me what my favorite spirit is, I always answer mezcal. Then they add: "Oh, yes, tequila!" At that point, I need to specify. "No, mezcal."

Tequila and mezcal might seem the same, but they are not. All tequilas are mezcals, but not all mezcals are tequilas, just as all cognacs are brandies, but not all brandies are cognacs. Mezcal and tequila differ in many ways, so let me give you a brief introduction to them.

In the pages that follow, we will see how mezcals (including tequila) are produced, from harvest to the bottle. We will see what types of mezcal and tequila you can find on the market so that you will know what to buy—and what not to buy. I will explain how these two spirits are regulated and trust me: they went through a lot before finally getting precise rules. Then we will have a quick look at the different agave types, or at least a selection of them. (There are myriad types of agave, and only a handful of them are used for the production of mezcal.) I dedicate a section to glassware, and what type of equipment you need in a home bar, and the professional-level techniques that you should master.

Last but not least, we will see how mezcal and tequila are drunk. Of course, the most popular way is drinking a shot with salt and lime, but believe it or not, that is not the Mexican way. In Mexico, mezcal is typically served neat with a little snack on the side and sipped. In this book, we take it a step further with over sixty of my absolute favorite classic and craft cocktails for mezcal and tequila.

Whether you are a professional bartender or a mezcal and tequila enthusiast, I hope this book will be useful to you. After you've read this book, who knows, maybe you will want to become a bartender, you will love mezcal and tequila as much as I do, and they will become your favorite spirits.

—*Emanuele Mensah*

THE HISTORY OF
MEZCAL AND TEQUILA

An intertwined story

Despite mezcal being a relatively new spirit in the market, mezcal and tequila have a history and tradition that stretch back at least four hundred years.

Everything started with mezcal. The name comes from the terms metls (agave) and ixcalli (cooked) in Nahuatl language. The agave was considered a sacred plant by the pre-Columbian tribes of Mexico, with a privileged position in religious rituals, mythology, and economy. It was nourishment, a water source, a fiber for making tools and clothing, food for animals, and a combustible for the village.

It was used to produce pulque, too: an alcoholic milky-colored beverage made from fermented agave juice, which appeared for the first time around the year 1000 AD. This milky liquid was so crucial to Aztecs that they even venerated two gods for the beverage's creation. One was Mayahuel, the goddess of the maguey, and the second was her husband Patecatl, the god of pulque. Its consumption was connected to religious rituals and reserved for certain social classes: it was used as a beverage when worshipping the goddess Mayahuel; during human sacrifices, it was given to those who were sacrificed to mitigate their suffering and drunk by the priests to stimulate their enthusiasm, and it was strictly forbidden for ordinary people.

It is not certain when the distillation process was first used in Mexico. According to one of the most common theories, when the Spanish started to colonize what is today Mexico, they brought with them a supply of their brandy from Europe. Once they drank it all, they had to find a substitute. Introduced to pulque, the Spanish, who knew the distillation process since the eighth century, started to experiment in order to make a higher alcohol content spirit, i.e., mezcal.

Alcohol consumption became strongly restricted, but after the conquest, drinking was no longer a taboo or a restriction, at least for a brief period. Since the Spanish introduced distillation and wine production, people started to refer to early versions of mezcal as Vino de Mezcal.

Mezcal and tequila were just a small hop away. In the early 1600s, Pedro Sánchez de Tagle, a nobleman who emigrated from Spain, built the first large-scale distillery based on the local agave plant's cultivation and production. Guess where? Exactly: Tequila, Jalisco (but, back then, the area was called New Galicia).

In 1698 mezcal was taxed, and quickly it spread from city to city. That is why, in 1640, the Spanish king forbade its production to promote the Spanish brandy. Around 1700, the spirit's demand increased drastically because of the Vino del Mezcal's good reputation. In 1795, when the Spanish king permitted José Antonio de Cuervo (who previously established an agave plantation in tequila and started to produce Vino del Mezcal) to sell the spirit, the modern tequila was born.

In the meantime, mezcal was very popular among soldiers during the Mexican War of Independence (1881–1821) but had a fall and had to wait for the recovery of the first republic to become a real and strong industry.

One of the stories tells that in 1873 Don Cenobio Sauza, one of the first tequila producers, changed the name from Vino de Mezcal to tequila in order to distinguish it from the mezcal produced in southern Mexico. Another theory says that when first exported, Vino de Mezcal was changed to Vino de Tequila and then shortened to tequila. And around 1873, when tequila appeared in the tax administration book, big mezcal producers asked the Mexican government permission to name the spirit tequila officially.

In the nineteenth century, the introduction of a new production method definitively established the difference between mezcal and tequila: from an underground process (which is still used for mezcal), producers developed an above-ground steam oven for tequila. With the new method, tequila got a milder flavor and became more suitable for a wider public, winning the prize at the Chicago World's Fair in 1893.

At the beginning of the twentieth century, producers started to sell tequila in bottles (instead of barrels), helping tequila to become the national pride. During the Mexican Revolution (1910–1920), tequila became the drink of freedom and progress.

Prohibition (1920–1933) made tequila even more popular, smuggled across the border in great quantities. And in 1935, with the creation of the margarita, tequila became indispensable both in Mexico and in the Western United States. After being advertised in radio and cinema as a macho drink in the 1980s, the real tequila boom exploded when American tourists in Mexico discovered the premium brands. That is when tequila finally made its way in bars. In the meantime, unfortunately, mezcal was pushed back, almost forgotten. Only in 2005 it was officially reintroduced and started its climb to success.

SO, WHAT IS MEZCAL? AND WHAT IS TEQUILA?

History being told, let us go a little bit deeper inside what mezcal and tequila really are. You already know the first rule: all tequilas are mezcals, but not all mezcals are tequilas.

Mezcal is a spirit obtained from the distillation of a fermented juice of agaves that have undergone a thermal treatment. It can be made from over thirty agave types (such as Tobalà and Espadín), and it must be produced in one of the nine different areas of Mexico (Durango, Guanajuato, Guerrero, Oaxaca, Puebla, Michoacán, San Luis Potosi, Tamaulipas, and Zacatecas). It must be certified by the Consejo Regulador del Mezcal (CRM). (See page 21 for regulation.)

Tequila is distilled from the Agave Tequiliana Weber Blue, or simply blue agave or Agave Azul (see page 25 on agave types) in only five areas of Mexico (Jalisco, Guanajuato, Michoacán, Nayarit, and parts of the State of Tamaulipas). In 1974, the Mexican government declared the term "tequila" as its intellectual property. It is illegal for other countries to produce or sell their own tequila (see page 21 on regulations).

HOW MEZCAL AND TEQUILA ARE MADE

So, how does agave get made into mezcal and tequila? It's an age-old process.

MEZCAL: FROM HARVESTING TO BOTTLING

Agave is the heart of mezcal, and every bottle is unique. That is because many factors influence mezcal, starting from the terroir. The soil, the climate, and the growing conditions (terroir) of a region are some of the reasons why mezcal differs from one to another.

Mexico has a great diversity in terms of soil types: desert, tropical areas, valleys, and mountains. Therefore, it has different microclimates that reflect on the spirit's taste and aroma. The agave that grows in a tropical area will have a different flavor from one that grows in a desert. Even the water used for fermentation is a factor of influence because whether that comes from a river, a creek, or a spring, it will have its own character that will affect mezcal.

LA COSECHA

The production process of mezcal starts with the harvesting *(cosecha)* of the agave. Small-scale producers handcraft mezcal, and each of them uses a method that has been passed down from generation to generation. Some are still using the same techniques practiced two hundred years ago.

Agave plants are perennial, but they mature and flower just once in their lifetime. When flowering, they grow a tall stem from the center called a *quiote*, which spreads the plant's seeds before it then dies. Agaves mature at different rates, depending on the variety of the plant, the soil nutrients, the access to water, and the climate. Generally speaking, it takes from seven to twelve years (but sometimes for up to thirty years) for the agave to ripen.

The harvesting success depends on selecting the raw materials and the jimador's experience. (A jimador is a mezcal master, and someone who manually harvests the agave in the fields.) He periodically checks the color of the leaves and the height of the stem.

When the agave plant nears the flowering point, the jimador cuts off the quiote so that all the sugars go to the piña, the heart of the agave from which mezcal and tequila are made. In this way, the plant continues to produce sugary sap to feed the stem, which is no longer there. The body of the plant swells and fills up with liquids. If the quiote is not noticed on time, then the plant, and therefore the piña, are unusable.

When the jimador understands that it is time, they cut off the plant's spiny leaves with a coa (a machete) until only the piña remains. Depending on the agave type, piñas can weigh anywhere from 40 to 200 pounds (20 to 90 kilograms).

EL HORNEADO

After the harvesting, the second step is the cooking (horneado) of the piñas. As much as the selected agave type, this process is another determining factor influencing the final product's flavor.

The most common method to cook agave is the palenque (pit in the ground), which has been used for hundreds of years. Not all the pits are the same, and they also differ in how the producers use them. Most palenques are cone-shaped and are about 10 feet wide (3 meters) at the top, tapering downward. People dig them in the ground, so their size can vary, determining how many piñas fit in the ground, the cooking time, and the mezcal flavor. Some palenques are lined with volcanic stones to ensure that the heat is intense and maintained for a long time. But since most of them are not lined, the piñas are in direct contact with the ground, which is why they need to be cooked for a longer time. This process will also affect the flavor of the mezcal.

Once the pit is dug, people ignite hardwood or coal and pile stones on and around it to hold in the heat. When the wood is completely burnt, and the stones are red hot, the piñas are placed into the pit on a layer of moist agave fibers, called bagaso, to protect them from the hot stones. Then the pile is covered with another layer of bagaso (or other types of fibrous material), and finally, the palenque is sealed with a thick layer of earth. It rests for three to five days to allow a complete and slow conversion of the carbohydrates into sugars. This is the stage where mezcal, due to the wood, smoke, and earth, gets its typical smokey flavor. After the steaming process, the oven is disassembled, and the piñas are stored in a clean and dry place.

LA MOLIENDA

Once the piñas are cooked, they need to go through the grinding process (molienda) to extract the juice and the sugar. The traditional method is called tahona (millstone). The mill wheel stands upright in a shallow basin containing the agave pieces and is connected to a central pole by a horizontal beam. The pole is pushed in circles, traditionally by a mule or a machine. But more often, due to financial reasons that don't allow the small producers to purchase a millstone or a mule, the piñas are grounded manually with a hammer. Only larger distilleries use a mechanical mill, but even this is rare.

LA FERMENTACIÓN

The fermentation process takes place outdoors. This means that the seasons, the weather conditions, the growing area, and the location where the fermentation occurs affect the process and, therefore, the final product.

After the piñas are grounded, the powder is placed in wooden barrels (another determining factor) with some water, and it is left to ferment. The barrels used can also be cemented cowhide-covered containers, large brick bowls, clay jugs, stainless steel tanks, hollowed-out rocks, and hollowed-out tree trunks. These containers are always open to allow for natural yeasts to begin fermentation.

The natural yeast converts the sugar into ethanol and other compounds that make mezcal. Sometimes chemicals, such as ammonium sulfate, are added to the juice to accelerate the fermentation. According to the weather, yeast type, and production technique, the process takes eight to twenty days. When all sugars are converted, the brew, called tepache, contains about 8% alcohol and is ready for distilling.

LA DESTILACIÓN

During the distillation, the alcohol is extracted from the fermented agave. Mezcal requires two distillations to reach its optimum alcohol volume (45%) and occasionally a third.

Traditionally, it is distilled in small kettles made from copper or clay. In the first case, we will get a fresh and crispy mezcal; in the second case, mezcal will have an earthy taste.

In the traditional method, a fire is burnt under the pot. A bowl of water is placed on the top of the pot, and when the fumes of the tepache hit the cool surface of the bowl, it turns into a liquid that is collected in a cup and channeled out of the kettle. The first alcohol, called heads, coming out from the copper kettle, contains many impurities, and so does the last alcohol, called tails. The heart, which is the pure mezcal between the heads and the tails, is used for the second distillation.

Mezcal distillers use a traditional method to determine the alcohol content and whether the mezcal needs to be distilled further: the venenciar. The distilled product is dropped into a small bowl (jicara) through a bamboo stick (venencia). Then the mezcal master looks for cordon de perlas (a string of pearls) around the edge of the jicara. If they are large and last for a long time, it means the alcohol content is 45%–55%.

PECHUGAS

Some producers distill mezcal with chicken breast (*pechuga*). After the second distillation, a third occurs with seasonal fruits and nuts, while a raw chicken breast is hung above the kettle. In this way, the fumes absorb the chicken's flavor before they condense into alcohol again. Some producers use turkey breast or rabbits or another type of meat, all known as pechugas. It is an expensive mezcal, and it is very traditional and distilled for family occasions or special days. This distillation's origin is not clear, but it is believed to be related to ancient sacrificial rituals when pulque was colored with chicken blood.

LA MADURACIÓN Y EL EMBOTELLAMIENTO

After the second distillation, mezcal can be bottled and consumed straight away, and called joven. But mezcal can also be aged in wooden barrels; in this case, it is called reposado or añejo. The first is aged for at least two months for up to one year; añejos are aged for at least one year.

TEQUILA: SIMILAR PROCESS, DIFFERENT PRODUCT

Tequila is made only from Agave Azul (see page 18 for agave types). It was first classified by German botanist F. Weber in 1905. It grows in rich and sandy soils in regions that generally did not have minimum temperatures below 24°F (-4°C) or maximum temperatures above 96°F (36°C) and at 5,000 feet (1,500 meters) of altitudes. The plant can reach over 7 feet (2 meters) in height and, once the quiote spread, it grows 16 feet (5 meters) more. The best period to plant the blue agave is when the rainy season starts, from June to September.

Agaves are grown in rows of one or two plants and, during the first two years, the space between the rows is used to cultivate other plants and thus supplement soil nutrients that nourish agaves. When the agave is seven to ten years old, then the harvest begins.

HARVEST

The jimadors, the experts in identifying a ripe agave, carry out the traditional harvesting method, which is centuries-old and passed down from generation to generation. Harvesting is not easy and requires keen eyes, good timing, and a jimador's acknowledgment.

They cut the leaves of the agaves with a coa de limpiar (a flat-bladed knife at the end of a long pole) without damaging the mother plant and agave until the whole heart is extracted from the ground. Only the heart, or piña, of the agave plant is used to make tequila. Then the piñas will be collected and transported to the distillery.

A mature agave can have leaves 5–8 feet (1.5–2.5 meters) tall and 7–12 feet (2–3.5 meters) in diameter. The average weight of the piña is around 80–200 pounds (35–90 kilograms). It has a lifespan of 6–14 years, depending on species, growing conditions, and climate. The older the agave, the longer the piña will accumulate the starches that will convert into fermentable sugars.

COOKING

Once harvested, the piñas are either halved or quartered and then placed in hornos de mampostería (masonry ovens) or in autoclaves (steel containers) to be steamed.

The steam process is quick in an autoclave and takes approximately 7–12 hours; in a horno de mampostería, it can take 36–72 hours.

These two processes serve the same purpose: softening the piñas and turning the natural starches and the complex carbohydrates of the agave into fermentable sugars suitable for fermentation.

GRINDING

After a short cooling period, the piñas are mashed to separate the pulp and fibers from the agave juice. This is done by shredding the agave and then crushing and washing the fibers with water.

Today there are three methods for extracting the juice: the tahona method, that is to say, a traditional milling stone turned by a horse or a donkey that pivots in a circular space to mash the cooked agave; the mechanical mill called molina, which is the most used by the producers; and the diffuser, used by large industrial producers, extracts the juice through steam and pressure.

FERMENTATION

The fermentation process is where the sugars and carbohydrates, naturally found in the agave, are converted into alcohol. Tequilas can be made with agave juice blended with 49% of sugar (which needs to be added before the fermentation process), or it can be made with 100% blue agave juice.

In the fermentation, yeast (any type, such as dry yeast or organic yeast) is added to the tequila blend or the blue agave juice; then the liquid, named mosto fresco, is mixed with water to be fermented in wooden barrels or stainless steel tanks. According to the types of yeast, climate, and the tank's volume, this process takes seven to twelve days.

Industrial tequila producers add nutrients and catalyzers, such as glycerine, to accelerate the fermentation. The chemical process heats the tanks, and the mosto fresco starts to bubble. When the bubbles disappear, the liquid, now called mosto muerto, is ready for distillation. Its ABV usually comes to 3%–5%.

DISTILLATION

Distillation is the process that separates alcohol from the fermented agave. Tequila is distilled twice (sometimes even three times) to reach the 35% alcohol content that it requires. Pot still, copper or stainless steel alembic, and column stills can be used.

The first distillation is called destroziamento and raises the alcohol content from 7% to 24%; the second is called rectificacíon and raises it to 55%.

During the destroziamento, the mosto muerto is added to the vessels and boiled, then the alcohol vapor is captured by the condenser and finally collected into a flask. The liquid that comes out of the still has three parts: the top is called the heads, the middle is the heart, and the bottom is the tails; the result of the first step is called ordinario.

During the rectificacíon, the heart is distilled a second time while the heads and tails are thrown away because they have the majority of the impurities.

After the final distillation, the heads and tails are once again removed, and the heart is sent on to barreling or bottling.

AGING AND BOTTLING

Tequila bottled straight after the distillation is called tequila blanco. If aged, tequila can be reposado (at least sixty days), añejo (at least twelve months), or extra añejo (at least three years; see page 18 for categories). The aging occurs in oak barrels (wooden barrels, called pipones, are also used for the reposado), often coming from the bourbon industry where barrels can only be used one time. Other barrels used include cognac barrels, sherry barrels, charred white oak barrels, and French oak. The type of barrel, how many times it has been used, its previous content, and how long tequila has been aged inside will influence the aroma, the flavor, and the color of the final product.

All Tequila 100% Agave must be bottled in Mexico with the description "Hecho en Mexico" (Made in Mexico). Tequila in bulk may be transported and bottled outside Mexico (see page 21 for regulations).

THE TYPES

Know your categories of mezcal and tequila

Certified mezcal is defined and classified by a Mexican government standard called the **Norma Oficial Mexicana (NOM)**. The NOM establishes three categories of mezcal: mezcal, artisanal mezcal, and ancestral mezcal. These three are broken down further into six classes: Blanco or Joven, Madurado en vidrio, Reposado, Añejo, Abocado, and Distilado con.

Mezcal is produced with modern production technologies imported from the tequila industry, such as an autoclave. A chemical engineer may take the master distiller's place as well. **Artisanal mezcal** includes the vast majority of certified mezcal. Modern technologies are prohibited; therefore, the mezcal is made by a master distiller and using traditional methods. **Ancestral mezcal** is a 100% traditional production. No additives or preservatives are used, and the agaves are only cooked in palenques. Fermentation is entirely natural, and distillation must be in clay pots (stainless steel is prohibited; see page 21 on regulations).

The subclasses, in terms of aging, are the following. **Blanco** or **joven** is unaged and unadulterated mezcal; **madurado en vidrio** (matured in glass) is a mezcal stored in glass for over twelve months, underground or with minimal light, temperature, and humidity. This is a method to soften the spirit without lowering the alcohol content. **Reposado** is aged for between two and twelve months while **añejo** is aged for at least one year. **Abocado** is a flavored or infused mezcal, including maguey worms, damiana, lime, orange, mango, and honey. The NOM permits herbs and caramels too. **Destilado con** (distilled with) is the third distillation done with other ingredients, such as regional fruits, meat, and herbs (see page 14 on pechugas).

PURISTS VS. PRAGMATISTS

There are two schools of thought: one followed by the purists, and the second by the pragmatists.

The purists belong to the Mezonte, a non-profit organization that promotes, supports, and preserves the traditional mezcal and distributes information about the spirit. They split mezcal into the three categories mentioned previously (industrial, artesanal, and traditional), and they have declared eight principles that mezcal must adhere to: the label must say 100% agave and indicate where the mezcal is from and what type of agave is used; the minimum alcohol content must be 45%; it must have bubbles when you shake the bottle; it should never be amber in color; if you can smell the aroma of mezcal on your hands and taste it at first sip, it's good mezcal.

Pragmatists also require a product made with 100% agave, with alcohol content between 36%–55%. The label should indicate origin, type of agave, and maestro mezcalero's name. Aged mezcals are accepted. The musts are: agave cooked in palenque, crushed by hand or with the tahona method, fermentation in open barrels with natural yeast, and distillation in copper or clay kettles. Industrialization is prohibited. Cocktails made with mezcal add value to the spirit; it does not need to be taken too seriously.

CATEGORIES OF TEQUILA: SILVER, JOVEN, AND GOLD

Unaged tequila is broken down into three categories. **Plata** or **silver** (**blanco** or **white**) is the purest form of tequila since it goes straight to the bottle without aging. Some producers allow the spirit to rest in stainless steel tanks for a short period (according to the regulation, no more than two months). This process makes the tequila smoother and easier to drink. Some other producers let the spirit age for six months, and that has created a new category, called suave, which identifies a very smooth tequila.

The second unaged category is **joven**, a 100% agave **blanco** tequila mixed with a **reposado** or **añejo** (in other words, a mixture of aged and unaged tequilas). **Oro**, **gold**, and **abocado** tequilas are always unaged but are not made from 100% agave; in fact, after distillation, **blanco** tequila is adulterated with coloring flavors, including caramel, glycerine, or wood chips to give it color and flavor. So, if the label states that it contains more than 0.5% additives, you will have a gold, oro, or abocado; if it is less than 0.5%, it is simply labeled as blanco.

Mixto is not a legal term, but it is used to label (not mandatory) tequilas not made from 100% blue agave but combined with other sugars, such as cane or high fructose corn syrup.

REPOSADO, AÑEJO, AND EXTRA AÑEJO

The place where tequila is aged is called a **bodega**, and it must be cool and dark. If the place is too warm and too dry, the barrels begin to dry out, and too much alcohol is lost (at least 5%–10% of alcohol is lost per year). But if the bodega is kept humid and the temperature is well regulated, then the loss can be limited to 2%–3% per year. Tequila is usually aged in American or French wooden barrels. A barrel's lifespan is approximately five years; after that, they don't exude any tannin, so they are destroyed or used for repairing other barrels.

Reposado is aged in barrels of 5,200 gallons (20,000 liters), called pipones, which ensures less contact with the wood and so less taste and color of it. The taste of reposado (aged for at least two months and at most one year) is richer and more complex than the tequila *blanco*.

Añejo is aged in barrels of 158 gallons (600 liters) maximum, but usually, they are smaller 34–52 gallons (130–200 liters); thus, the tequila comes often in contact with the wood, absorbing the taste and the color of the wood. Some producers use new barrels to get a woodier taste and color. Añejo is aged between one to three years and has a complex aroma with a noticeable agave note left.

The extra añejo category was introduced in 2006 to compete with other spirits that are aged for a longer period. Extra añejo is aged between three to five years in similar barrels as the añejo. The maximum volume is 158 gallons (600 liters), but more often a 52–66 gallons (195–250 liters) volume barrels are used. A good extra añejo should have an intense color, and it should be very mild, balanced, and complex.

REGULATIONS

Main regulations for mezcal and tequila

In 1994 the first official regulation for mezcal was established, NOM-070-SCFI-1994, saying that mezcal must meet certain requirements for its production, packaging, and commercialization. In 1995, mezcal got the Appellation of Origin (Domination of Origin in Spanish or D.O.), it wasn't until 2005 that the official law came into effect and required that all mezcal be certified. The D.O., which sets the quantities and standards of mezcal production, provides a guideline and a database regarding agave plantations, wild agaves, cultivated land, how every mezcal distillery produces its mezcal, and what type of agave is used. In 1997 an inspection body, called Consejo Mexicano Regolador de la Calidad del Mezcal (previously COMERCAM, today C.M.R.) was created to check that all mezcal complies with the NOM regulations.

There are many NOM regulations, but the major ones are as follows: Mezcal must be made in one of the nine specified regions (Oaxaca, Guerrero, Durango, San Luis Potosi, Zacatecas, Guanajuato, Tamaulipas, Michoacan, and Puebla); mezcal must be made with 100% agave (previously, up to 20% of other carbohydrate spirits like sugarcane or corn were allowed); mezcal can be made with any agave but must be cooked before the fermentation process and bottled between 36–55% ABV; bottles must be labeled with "100% Maguey" or "100% Agave," the C.M.R. logo, the word "mezcal," the type of agave used, the registered brand (as well as the name, address, and official NOM number of the producer), and the number of the batch; "Made in Mexico" or the Eagle's Head symbol must indicate that the spirit was produced in Mexico within the demarcated region and according to all laws and regulations; mezcal may not be exported in bulk and must be bottled in a distillery. Mezcal can belong to one of three categories: mezcal, artisanal mezcal, and ancestral mezcal. And there are six subcategories: blanco, reposado, anejo, madurado en vidro, distillado con, or abocado (see page 18 for more on categories).

	Cooking	Milling	Fermentation	Distillation
Mezcal	Palenque (pit in the ground), horno de mamposteria (brick kiln)	Tahona, Chilean or Egyptian mill (both a variant of tahona), el trapiche (Mexican sugar mill), molina (mechanical mill), or other mills.	Wooden containers, masonry basins (concrete or earthen tanks), or stainless steel tanks.	Alembic pot still, continuous/column stills made of copper or stainless steel.
Mezcal Artesanal	Palenque (pit in the ground), Horno de mamposteria (brick kiln)	Hand mallet, a tahona, a Chilean or Egyptian mill, el trapiche (Mexican sugar mill), molina (mechanical mill)	Animal skins, pits, or tanks made of stone, earth, tree trunk, masonry basins (concrete or earthen tanks), or wood. Fibers of the agave may be used in the process.	With direct fire under the copper stills or clay pots, condensing coil from wood, clay, or stainless steel. Fibers of the agave may be used in the process.
Mezcal Ancestral	Palenque	Hand mallet, tahona, Chilean or Egyptian mill.	Animal skins, pits, or tanks made of stone, earth, tree trunk, masonry basins (concrete or earthen tanks), or wood. Fibers of the agave must be used in the process.	With direct fire under clay pots, condensing coil from wood or clay. Fibers of the agave must be used in the process.

MAIN REGULATIONS FOR TEQUILA

In 1949, due to the high demand for tequila and the increased production of poor-quality products, the Mexican government established a monitoring division, called the Norma Official Mexicana (NOM), to monitor the producers, to delimit agricultural areas, and to establish that tequila has to be made with 100% agave. In 1974 the *General Declaration For Protection of the Appellation Of Origin Tequila* (D.O.T.) was published to ensure that tequila is produced only in designated areas. In Mexico, tequila, mezcal, bacanora, and sotol have the Appelation of Origin. In 2006, the Appellation of Origin for tequila was included in the list of UNESCO World Heritage Sites. The designated areas where tequila may be produced are Jalisco (the entire state), Guanajuato (seven cities), Michoacán (30 cities), Nayarit (eight cities), and Tamaulipas (eleven cities).

The criteria of the Appellation of Origin (an international agreement issued by the World Intellectual Property Organization in accordance with the Lisbon Agreement) are:

1) The name must contain the geographical entity of the country of origin;
2) The geographical name must be an indication of the place where the product was originally created;
3) The product must originate from the natural and cultural heritage of a specific area.

In 1976 a distinction was made between tequila made of 100% agave (premium) and tequila made of 51% agave, and in 1994 the Consejo Regulador del Tequila (C.R.T.) was created to check that all tequila producers meet NOM requirements. Only if the tequila meets the criteria, can it get a certificate and be sold. In 1997 the European Union signed a commercial accord to recognize Mexico as the only producer of tequila.

Legally, tequila is protected by three laws: Ley Federal de Metrologia y Normalizacíon (Art. 52, 68,69, 73), the regulation for measuring techniques and standardization, and Normas oficiales Mexicanas. Internationally, Mexico signed a trade agreement with other countries to protect tequila. These countries, which may only import and sell tequila with an Appellation of Origin, are Bolivia, Colombia, Costa Rica, Ecuador, the United States, Canada, European Union, Israel, Japan, and China.

NORMA OFFICIAL MEXICANA

The NOM is the official Mexican standard for tequila and protects the origin of the name, regulates the production, and sets the standards to guarantee the quality. These standards include all processes related to the cultivation of agave, production, marketing, information, and commercial activities. Every bottle requires a NOM number that refers to the distillery where the tequila was produced; thus, it is very easy to trace a specific tequila's origin (but not the origin of the agave).

The most important regulations of the NOM are:
1) Tequila must be made from the Agave Tequiliana Weber Azul;
2) Tequila must be produced in one of the five designated regions;
3) At least 51% of the alcohol content must be originated from blue agave;
4) The alcohol content must be 35%–55%

The NOM divides tequila into two categories:
1) Tequila must contain at least 51% Agave Tequiliana Weber Azul and may contain 49% sugar. It may be sold in bulk and bottled outside Mexico;
2) 100% agave tequila is 100% Agave Tequiliana Weber Azul tequila. It is bottled only in Mexico, and the Consejo Regulador del Tequila monitors it.

Both categories are divided into five other types: blanco, jove, reposado, añejo, and extra añejo. The label on the tequila bottles intended for export must state:
1. The word *tequila*;
2. To which category they belong;
3. Additives (from 0.5%);
4. Net volume;
5. Alcohol content (35%–55%);
6. Name, address, NOM number of the producer;
7. The registered brand;
8. "Hecho en Mexico" (made in Mexico);
9. Number of the batch;
10. Information regarding health upon excessive consumption.

ALL ABOUT AGAVE

An illustrious plant

The term agave was initially used by the Taíno, an Indian tribe from the Caribbean Island. In the sixteenth century, the Spanish conquerors started to call agave maguey, and, later on, in 1753, a Swedish botanist, Carl Linnaeus, renamed maguey plant agave in his book *Species Plantarum*. Agave, from Greek mythology "the illustriousness of the nobility," is the botanical name for a genus of succulent plants that belong to the Agavaceae family.

Over 300 species of agave have been described, but only 200 are currently recognized. Agave plants grow only in a dry subtropical climate, and they are native to southern parts of North America, Central America, West Indies, and northern parts of South America. They exist in a wide range of sizes and colors. Most species are monocarpic (they flower once, then die), but a few can bloom several times during their lives. They grow slowly and blossom only after many years (15–20 years). They sprout little clones of themselves from their bases; these are most commonly called hijuelos.

Most agaves have rosettes of thick, hard, and succulent leaves with marginal teeth and, usually, with a sharp terminal spine. Flower spikes range from 8 feet (2.5 meters) to as tall as 60 feet (18 meters) high on the large varieties. They tolerate well-draining soil but favor rocky or sandy soil. They can go without water for weeks.

During the day, the agaves close their pores to prevent dehydration and use sunlight to create chloroplasts. At night, the pores open, and the agaves absorb CO_2. As already mentioned, tequila can be made only with blue agave. However, mezcal is produced with different agaves. In fact, local producers use the agave found in their vicinity, which is generally called Silvestre on the bottle. Some producers blend various types of agaves, which are labeled as "Ensemble."

It is quite impossible to list every agave species. The most commonly used are as follows.

AGAVE TEQUILIANA WEBER AZUL

The Agave Tequiliana Weber Azul takes its name from a sort of blue layer on the fleshy leaves, which are rich in fibers and can reach a length of up to 6.5 feet (2 meters).

Once flowered, the blue agave sprout a stalk (called quiote) which has branches with small yellow flowers and small agaves, called bulbillos. These sometimes fall and grow further on the ground. It does not happen in cultivated agave fields because the quiote is always cut down.

The flowers, pollinated by the greater long-nosed bat (also by insects and hummingbirds), produce thousands of seeds. It usually takes 15–20 years for the agave blue to bloom.

The high production of sugars, mainly fructose, in the plant's core is the main characteristic that makes the agave suitable for tequila production.

AGAVE ANGUSTIFOLIA ESPADÍN

This is the most common agave, and almost 90 percent of mezcal is made with it. Espadín, a genetic ancestor of the Agave Tequiliana Weber Azul and one of the varieties of the A. Angustofilia, is a medium-size agave with sawtooth edges and a sharp point. It can reach up to 12 feet (4 meters), and its piña weighs up to 220 pounds (100 kg). It takes about eight to twelve years to mature, the reason why it is the most used plant for producing mezcal. Espadín gives citrus and roasted agave notes to the final product.

AGAVE MARMORATA TEPEZTATE

Part of the Agave Marmorata family, Agave Tepeztate is found in the wilderness and takes up to thirty years to ripen. It grows on dry soil like rocks on the mountains' slopes, and it is one of the longest living agaves since it can live almost for twenty years. When it blossoms, it produces rich yellow flowers at the top of a small stem. It can grow quite big and has a distinct, erratic leaf structure. It is mildly toxic; in fact, you can develop an allergic reaction if you get pricked by its sharp points. Tepeztate gives a sweet taste, with summer citrus notes to the mezcal.

AGAVE POTATORUM TOBALÁ

This species grows at higher elevations (around 5,000 feet, 1,500 meters) and prefers rocky canyons and very shady ground. It is much smaller in size than traditional agaves, and it is harder to procure because it does not produce offspring on its own. Birds and bats pollinate and spread its seeds. Tobalá has broad spade-like leaves, and it takes twelve to fifteen years to bloom. Mezcal made from Tobalá tends to be fruity and complex.

AGAVE KARWINSKII

Barril, Madrecuixe, Tobaziche, and Cuixe are all sub-species of the Agave Karwinskii family. It may be difficult to understand which one is used for a specific mezcal as the names often change due to many dialects. This species grows vertically with a cylindrical, stalk-shaped piña and the leaves spreading at the top. It is a wild agave that grows mainly in a dry and low-lying area; it does not produce offspring, counting the propagation on its rhizome system. The plant is harvested at fifteen years old and offers an herbaceous and savory flavor.

AGAVE AMERICANA VAR. OAXACENSIS ARROQUEÑO

Arroqueño is considered the genetic mother of the Agave Espadín and it is native to the Oaxaca Central Valley. It has leaves that can span as wide as 10 feet (3 meters) and takes up to twenty-five years to reach maturity.

It is an endangered species as mezcal's popularity rises (because of the extensive time required for this agave to grow). A few producers are doing sustainability projects to plant new Arroqueño in the Oaxacan hills. It gives floral and vegetal notes.

AGAVE DURANGENSIS CENIZO

Typically found outside of Oaxaca, Cenizo is the most common agave used in Durango and Zacatecas. It grows at high altitudes (between 5,500 and 8,500 feet, or 1600 and 2500 meters) in cold, dry conditions. Cenizo is one of the most fibrous agave varieties, and it can take nine to thirteen years to mature. It provides an herbal and earthy taste.

HOW TO DRINK MEZCAL

There is no wrong way to drink mezcal, here I have outlined best practices for each.

PURE

To enjoy mezcal and tequila, you must try the pure method. First of all, you need to be sure that the spirit is at room temperature, then pour 1 ounce into a snifter (see page 32 about glassware), or even better, into a Riedel Ouverture Tequila Glass, chosen by the Consejo Regulador del Tequila as the ultimate glass for tasting and drinking tequila. Remember to avoid ice because it will be difficult to taste tequila and mezcal's subtle flavor. Then take the first sip: it needs to be small, and you need to take your time to get used to the taste. So let the mezcal reach each part of your mouth, tongue, palate, and gums. If you don't, the spirits just will burn your mouth, and you won't be able to taste them. After the warm-up of the first sip, smell the aroma of the tequila or mezcal. After that, swirl the spirit in the glass to aerate it and gather the aroma at the glass's edge. Smell it twice and then take a sip and let tequila or mezcal roll in your mouth and rest a bit on the tongue to discover other flavors. Then swallow and enjoy the aftertaste.

SHOTS

Mezcal is rarely drunk in shots; it is meant to be sipped slow and savored. The only way you can drink mezcal in a shot (but again, even in this case, we are talking about sips) is with sal de gusano, meaning a mix of ground-up red worms, salt, and chili pepper. Occasionally Mexicans dip a slice of orange or pineapple in a bowl of sal de gusano in order to get a blast of fruit tempered with the salty and umami flavor of the sal de gusano. Outside Oaxaca, where it is almost sold for free, sal de gusano is pretty expensive. Still, it is an incredible experience.

Mezcal is served in copitas (shallow clay cups with a wide opening on the top so that it is easier to get all the complexities of the mezcal) or jicaras, made of natural plant fibers from the fruits of the Calabash tree.

It is more common to drink tequila in shots. The Western way of putting salt on the back of the hand, licking it up, swallowing the shot, and sucking a slice of lime comes from Mexico. In 1928, due to a flu epidemic, doctors prescribed their patients tequila with salt and lime. Although the Western way is still done with blanco tequila and by young people on a night out, Mexicans prefer to sip the spirit and dip a slice of lime in salt and suck on it until the glass is empty.

SANGRITA AND BANDERA

Sangrita, which means "small blood" in Spanish, is a sweet and spicy mixture to sip alongside a tequila shot to enhance the spirit's flavor and clean the palete between every sip. Its origins are not clear (probably Chapala Lake in Jalisco), and, nowadays, there are many recipes and commercial mixes. Generally speaking, sangrita is made with leftover orange juice, pomegranate juice, chili powder, and other spices. Some American recipes include tomato juice or Worcestershire sauce, but more traditional Mexican versions have citrus as the dominant character.

Bandera (flag) is another way to drink tequila (never mezcal). Inspired by the colors of their flag, Mexicans take a sip of the lime juice (which represents the green), then a sip of tequila (white), and finally a sip of sangrita (red). In Mexico, bandera is traditionally served in a caballito, a narrow shot glass.

COCKTAILS

If you are not a sipper, mezcal and tequila are great spirits for your cocktails. The most famous tequila-based cocktail is probably the margarita, but both of these spirits can be used in so many ways. Keep reading, and you will be introduced to and amazed by the magical world of mezcal and tequila cocktails.

GUSANO DEL MAGUEY

Gusano del Maguey is, contrary to popular belief, not a worm but a moth larva that is found on the agave plant and is harmful. There are two types of larvae: meocuiles, which are white butterfly caterpillars, and chilocuiles, which are red moth larva. They don't measure the spirit's alcohol content or give a hallucinatory effect, but they are quite popular in Mexican cuisine.

Many theories explained how a "worm" ended up in a bottle of mezcal. One of them is that in the 1950s, to attract more attention, some producers came up with the idea to put a worm into mezcal bottles. This trick worked with tourists, and many other producers followed the experiment. But that was bad mezcal, and in the end, US tourists got used to poor-quality mezcal, which had a worm stuck in it.

This bad reputation lasted for almost fifty years. In 1995, some mezcal producers began a movement to ban the worm against those who thought that, since it became a kind of urban mythology, North American buyers would have rejected non-worm-mezcals. The Mexican Health Department decided that worms were safe for human consumption and allowed them to stay in the bottle.

Nowadays, we know that tequila can't be made with worms but that it is still possible to find them in some mezcal bottles—but not good mezcal bottles.

PULQUE, BACANORA, RAICILLA, AND SOTOL: THE WONDERFUL WORLD OF AGAVE

The agave plant is not used only for producing mezcal and tequila. Other spirits are distilled from this plant full of resources.

Let us talk a little bit about **pulque** again (see page 8). We already know the importance of pulque in pre-Colombian Mexico. A cornerstone of religious rituals and an essential social element, it was drunk by the elite in Indian civilizations. Only after the Spanish conquest did it become a more accessible drink.

It has a low ABV (5%–7%), and it is made with agave sap (approximately ten different agave types). Aguamiel (the sap) gathers at the center of the plant's leaves and is produced near the end of the agave's life, reaching 158 gallons (600 liters). The sap, collected with a steel scoop or a bucket, is fermented in a cask. The fermentation is quick (four to thirteen days), and there is no distillation. The flavor is sour, yeasty, and slightly viscous. Unfortunately, it is only sold in Mexico.

- **Bacanora** can only be made with Agave Pacifica (Agave Angustifolia var. Pacifica) that grows in Sonora's high mountains (it is indeed named after the town Bacanora in Sonora state). It was illegal from 1915 to 1992 because Sonora's governor was very religious and producing or drinking alcohol was considered immoral. But in 2000, Bacanora was finally regulated by the Mexican government, and in 2006, Consejo Sonorense Promotor de la Regulacion del Bacanora was founded. Like mezcal, the piñas are cooked in palenques to give a typical smoky flavor. Then, after being crushed, it is fermented in the open air and distilled twice.

- **Raicilla** is an herbal distillate produced exclusively in the Western part of Jalisco. It is made from Agave Maximiliana (also called Agave Pata de Mula) and Agave Inaequidens (also called Agave Lechuguilla). After the harvesting, piñas are roasted above ground, fermented (for 30 days), and distilled in tabernas (Raicilla distilleries) by raicilleros (the distillers). It is not supported yet by the Norma Oficial Mexicana, but in 2019 got the Denomination of Origin. Since it is usually cooked above ground, Raicilla does not have the same smoky flavor as mezcal; it is more fragrant than tequila.

- **Sotol** refers both to the plant and the spirit. It can be produced only in three northern states: Chihuahua, Coahuila, and Durango. It is made from Dasylirion Wheeleri (also called the desert spoon), which, in the past, was considered an agave plant. But in the '90s, it was reclassified under the Nolinaceae family. From that point on, sotol has not been considered mezcal anymore. In 2004 it got the Mexican Denomination of Origin (it does not extend beyond Mexico so other countries can produce it), and the Consejo Mexicano de Sotol was founded to regulate the production of sotol. The piñas are usually cooked above ground for several days, then crushed, fermented in open air, and distilled in a column or pot still. The flavor of sotol may vary from fresh herbs notes, such as eucalyptus, if the plant grew in a forest area, to earthy notes if the plant is desert-born.

ESSENTIAL GLASSWARE

As previously mentioned, mezcal and tequila are best served in Riedel Ouverture Tequila Glasses, copitas jicaras, or caballitos (see page 28) when sipping them. But when combined with other ingredients, such as spirits or syrups, to make cocktails, a whole new world opens up.

Even if the glassware is not the most essential aspect of a drink, it should be elegant and sparkling clean in order to show that the appropriate attention to detail went into the drink. Each type of cocktail glass is designed to bring out the complexities in the aroma, temperature, color, and flavor of the drink.

Specific glasses are required for certain cocktails, such as martini or a piña colada. You will never see a martini served in a highball or a piña colada in a rocks glass. But this doesn't mean that you need to buy a complete set of glassware, especially if you just want to make cocktails at home for yourself and your friends. If you choose wisely, you will be able to buy a few and cover an entire category of cocktails. In fact, besides a few classic cocktails, all the others can easily be used for an extensive range of drinks. Keep in mind that when you choose a glass, you need to think about the characteristics of your drink and the appropriate vessel that will suit it. If your cocktail is served cold and without ice, you will want something with a stem so that the hand does not warm the drink.

But don't worry, many glasses can be used for dual purposes, and you do not need to buy too many to make great cocktails at home.

GLASSWARE	SERVING	CATEGORY	DESCRIPTION
absinthe fountain and absinthe glasses	Fountains come with 1, 2, 4, or 6 taps. The capacity of each glass is 8–11 ounces.	sipping liqueur and fortified wine	Absinthe fountains first appeared in bars in the late 1800s, when absinthe became popular. They were used to dispense water. You have complete control over the drink flow with the fountain, from a steady stream to a gentle drip. It is excellent for sharing cocktails at parties; you just need to add as many Absinthe Glasses as you want and which typically are tall, with wide rims, a dose line, and a bulge or bubble to indicate how much absinthe to pour.
beer mugs	10–14 ounces	beer line	With mugs, you can hold onto your beer without warming it with your hands. Beer mugs come in a variety of shapes and sizes.
brandy snifters	5–8 ounces	sipping liqueur and fortified wine	Used to enjoy bourbon, brandy, and whiskey, snifters are designed to make it easy for drinkers to grasp the cup in their hand and transfer heat to drinks—like brandy—that are best served at room temperature. The round bowl is also designed to swirl and sniff the drink while consuming it.
champagne flutes	6–8 ounces	wine	Champagne flutes are an excellent addition to your glassware collection for quite a few reasons: not only can you find beautiful flutes, but also the design maintains the drink's carbonation and allows the bubble to travel further to the top of the glass. A heads-up: store your flutes in the freezer before serving and when pouring champagne, remember to hold the glass at a 45-degree angle and fill it to half its capacity.

GLASSWARE	SERVING	CATEGORY	DESCRIPTION
coupe glasses	6–8 ounces	wine	Also known as a champagne saucer, the coupe glass is not used as much as the popular champagne flute and the tulip glass. It was quite common back in the early 1900s when it was easy to drink the syrup-based champagne from the wide and shallow cup. The bowl's shape doesn't allow it to maintain bubbles; that's why it is used to serve craft cocktails, such as the cosmopolitan, clover club, and Bronx.
champagne tulips	6–8 ounces	wine	A champagne tulip has a broader bowl than a champagne flute so that you can enjoy the aroma of the bubbles. A slight curve characterizes the glass allowing concentrated aeration and the bubble to rise. You can use it for cocktails such as French 75, Bellini, and Death in the Afternoon.
Collins glasses	8–12 ounces	cocktails and mixed drinks	Collins glasses are cylindrical and an excellent alternative to highball glasses. These two are quite similar, but highballs are shorter and skinnier. Collins glasses are typically used for cocktails such as Tom Collins and John Collins.
copita or sherry glasses	3–4 ounces	sipping liqueur and fortified wine	The copita (or sherry glass) was traditionally used for sherry, but many use it nowadays for aromatic alcoholic beverages, such as port, liqueurs, and whisky. That is because the narrow and relatively tall size keeps the aromas concentrated.

GLASSWARE	SERVING	CATEGORY	DESCRIPTION
cordial glasses	2–3 ounces	sipping liqueur and fortified wine	These are small and stemmed glasses generally used for after-dinner liqueurs. But you can use them in many other ways, such as at parties or receptions. Cordial glasses are also known as pony glasses, but that is incorrect: a pony glass is not stemmed, despite holding the same amount of liquid.
coupettes	4–8 ounces	cocktails and mixed drinks	According to an urban myth, the coupette was molded in the shape of Marie Antoinette's left breast. But the truth is the glass was invented in England in 1663, long before the queen. Store coupettes in the freezer before using them.
Glencairn whisky glasses	3–5 ounces	sipping liqueur and fortified wine	Coming into production in 2011, the Glencairn whisky glass features a tulip-shaped bowl that sits on a sturdy base, helping to directly deliver the beverage's aroma to the drinker's nose. The glass has three variations: the 24 percent lead crystal version, the lead-free crystal version, and the soda-lime version, which is the most common.
grappa glasses	2–4 ounces	sipping liqueur and fortified wine	The grappa glass is designed specifically for the high-alcohol Italian beverage. Since grappa is sensitive to temperature, the glass features a long stem that prevents heat transfer.

GLASSWARE	SERVING	CATEGORY	DESCRIPTION
highball glasses	8–10 ounces	cocktails and mixed drinks	Tall and narrow, highball glasses are very versatile. You can use them for high cocktails like the paloma, but also, you can build a drink directly into the glass, such as an easy to make and tasteful gin and tonic.
hurricane and poco grandes glasses	8–10 ounces	cocktails and mixed drinks	Hurricanes and poco grandes are taller and broader than highballs. They have a tulip style shape with a stem from where you can hold the glass and allow the cocktails not to get warm. There is a small difference between hurricanes and poco grandes: the latter is shallower, with a longer stem yet slightly shorter in size.
Irish coffee glasses	8–10 ounces	cocktails and mixed drinks	Irish coffee glasses are made of glass, a thick stem, and a sturdy base that holds up a narrow bowl. The rim on top ensures the toppings stay in place, such as whipped cream. They are mostly used for hot beverages and boozy hot chocolates.
julep cups	12–13 ounces	cocktails and mixed drinks	The julep is a short conical-shaped cup, commonly in stainless steel but sometimes made of silver or pewter. You need to store it in the freezer, but do not worry, if you forgot, when at room temperature, the ice still chills the cup, forming a thick frost and coating the outside of the cup. Commonly used for the mint julep and all its twists.

GLASSWARE	SERVING	CATEGORY	DESCRIPTION
martini glasses	3–6 ounces	cocktails and mixed drinks	The martini glass was introduced as an alternative to the coupe glass and was initially used for serving champagne. Nowadays, the glass has a long stem to minimize heat transfer and a wide brim to intensify the aromas. The sides are steeply sloped, which helps to support the garnish. A martini glass can be used for drinks served up, such as the Gibson, Tuxedo, and espresso martini.
copper mugs, a.k.a. mule mugs	12 ounces	cocktails and mixed drinks	Copper mugs, associated with Moscow Mule mugs, can instantly turn and remain cold, and that's why they typically have a handle to minimize the transmission of heat. They originally were and still are used to serve Moscow Mule cocktails. Cold copper tends to increase the number of bubbles in ginger beer, giving great fizziness.
Nick-and-Nora glasses	4–6 ounces	cocktails and mixed drinks	The Nick-and-Nora glass is named after a fictional couple created in the novel (and film) *The Thin Man* by Dashiell Hammett, and the specific style of cocktail glasses they drink out of. Nick is a booze-soaked private detective, and his wife Nora is a Nob Hill heiress. The glass is used for drinks served up, such as Manhattan, Hanky Panky, and Little Italy. You can hold the glass from the stem, avoiding transmitting heat. Despite this, it's still always a good idea to chill it in the freezer before use.

GLASSWARE	SERVING	CATEGORY	DESCRIPTION
old-fashioned glasses, a.k.a. rocks glasses, a.k.a. lowball glasses	6–10 ounces	cocktails and mixed drinks	Named after the classic old-fashioned, this glass is also known as the rocks glass or lowball glass. It is short, with a wide rim and thick base so that you can muddle non-liquid ingredients directly inside the glass. Designed to serve whisky, nowadays you can use it for cocktails too. A double old-fashioned (also known as a DOF) glass is simply a double-sized rocks glass with a capacity of 12–16 ounces.
punch bowl and punch cups	variable	cocktails and mixed drinks	A punch bowl is a large and wide bowl used for serving punch. The first appearance of punch dates back to 1632 in India, and the drink was made of spirits, sugar, lemon, water, or teas and spices. Early punch bowls were made of ceramic or silver and often elaborate. After a period of popularity in England and in the New World, people stopped using them. Nowadays, punch bowls have acquired fame again. Punch cups are used to serve a small quantity of strong drinks. Cocktails are first mixed in the punch bowl and then poured into cups.
red wine glasses	8–12 ounces	wine	The large round bowl of a red wine glass increases oxidation and smooths out the consistency, taste, and aroma. The rim tends to be narrowed so that the wine's smell and taste can be directed to the drinker's nose. You can use red wine glasses not only for wines but for Sangria and spritzes as well.

GLASSWARE	SERVING	CATEGORY	DESCRIPTION
shot glasses	1.5–3 ounces	sipping liqueur and fortified wine	Shot glasses are great for quick and straight consumption of liquors. They can be dropped in cocktails as well. They are short, small, and narrow, and they come in all shapes and sizes. The two common measures are: single (1.05 ounces) and double (2–3 ounces).
sling glasses	11 ounces	cocktails and mixed drinks	Similar to a Pilsner beer glass, a sling glass is perfect for long cocktails. It is tall and elegant and named after the drink Singapore Sling. It features a short stem on a wide foot and a thick base in the bowl.
sour glasses	3–6 ounces	cocktails and mixed drinks	Sour glasses were introduced in the middle of the nineteenth century when the mix of a spirit, sweetener, and citrus juices wouldn't fit a rocks glass. A sour glass has a rounded cup, slanted sides, and a narrow stem that helps keep a cold drink. You can use it for straight-up sour drinks, such as Whisky Sour.
teacups	6–8 ounces	cocktails and mixed drinks	Teacups are commonly used for drinking tea, but lately, they are turning into fashion vessels to serve chilled cocktails. They are typically glass cups on the top of porcelain saucers or porcelain cups on glass stems.

GLASSWARE	SERVING	CATEGORY	DESCRIPTION
tiki mugs	14–22 ounces	cocktails and mixed drinks	Tiki mugs are ceramic drinking vessels decorated with Polynesian idols and tropical themes. The most common ones are shaped with Easter Island statues, but tiki mugs come in all sizes and shapes.
toddy glasses	8.5 ounces	cocktails and mixed drinks	A toddy glass has a stem or a handle to allow the drinker to hold it comfortably. A toddy glass needs to be heated with hot water before use. It is generally used for hot toddy cocktails and their twists.
white wine glasses	8–13 ounces	wine	The white wine glass stem is smaller and shorter than the red one, since generally, white wines have a lighter profile. Another difference: the rim is not narrowed for less oxidation and more crispiness in the flavor. White wine glasses are used for spritzes and wine-based cocktails.
Zombie glasses	10–12 ounces	cocktails and mixed drinks	Like a Collins glass, the Zombie glass has been designed for the Zombie cocktail but is now used for long drinks. It is generally taller and larger than most glasses to highlight the color of the drink.

KEY EQUIPMENT
AND TECHNIQUES

*It doesn't take much to set up an excellent home bar if you have a few key tools—
and a handful of techniques under your belt.*

EQUIPMENT: FROM THE ESSENTIALS TO NICE LITTLE PERKS

The first step to making cocktails at home for yourself and your friends is
mastering the bar equipment. This is as important as learning new cocktail
recipes. Today, due to more precision and increased skill among bartenders, you
can find a wide variety of bar tools on the market.

If you just started to experiment with recipes and cocktails, you need to
know that there are a few essential tools that you need to invest in. With them,
you will be able to make a good range of cocktails. Then, if you become quite
passionate about the bar world, you can buy a few more tools that will let you
experiment a little bit more with new recipes.

Of course, if you don't have a shaker, you can use a thermos flask or a
protein shaker instead. And in place of a jigger, you can measure with spoons
and cups. But below, you can find a list of essential tools—plus the fancy ones
that will please the bartender soul in you!

SHAKERS: BOSTON, COBBLER, AND PARISIAN

The shaking process introduces tiny air bubbles into the mixture, giving
the right texture to the drink. It also rapidly chills and dilutes the cocktail.
In approximately 12–15 seconds of shaking, the drink will reach thermal
equilibrium, meaning it will not get any colder. Temperature and dilution are
critical when you make a drink, and they are related: the colder the drink is, the
less it dilutes.

Archaeological evidence shows that drinks were mixed in large vessels
back in 7000 BC. But, likely around the mid-nineteenth century, shakers
became a bartenders' tool when, the theory says, someone in a bar put various

sized vessels together, shook the contents, and obtained a slightly different flavor compared to a simple rolling.

The main three shakers are Boston, cobbler (or three-piece shaker), and Parisian (a.k.a. Parisienne or French). A **Boston shaker** is suitable for both beginners and experienced bartenders. It consists of two pieces: a mixing glass (usually sixteen ounces capacity, or 175 milliliters) that should come tempered, and a slightly larger, flat-bottomed stainless steel cone (twenty-eight ounces, or 800 ml). There are also tin-on-tin varieties. The metal part fits over the glass during the shaking process. The glass part enables you to see the ingredients as you work. The Boston shaker is the typical bartenders' choice because you can make up to three cocktails at once, and it is faster to shake. (For more on how to use it, see page 55.)

The **cobbler shaker** was invented in 1884 by Edward Hauck by adding a strainer to the French shaker's cap. It comes in various sizes, and it looks classier than the Boston shakers. It consists of a tight-fitting cap (which works as a jigger and measures 1 ounce, or 28 milliliters) covering a strainer built in a metal cone. The cap and the lid seal tightly, but it may be difficult for beginners to use a cobbler because, as it chills, the metal contracts and can make it quite difficult for the three parts to separate after shaking. The built-in shaker has large holes, so a cobbler is not recommended when you need to strain through a fine mesh.

The **Parisian shaker** is a two-piece set of two stainless steel tins that fit tightly together; they require more time when you need to separate them. It is a stylish shaker but not used so much behind bars, although it has been around for centuries; in fact, it is often called "the original shaker." It can be described as halfway between the Boston shaker and the cobbler shaker. The cap of the French shaker sits inside the cup, giving a better seal than the cobbler and making it less likely to freeze shut.

STRAINERS: HAWTHORNE, JULEP, AND FINE MESH

Cocktail strainers allow us to separate the ice used to shake or stir the drink and to have more control over the dilution process. If you are using a Boston shaker or a French one, the second essential tool you will need is a strainer. There are three types of strainers, and all of them have a different aim.

The **Hawthorne strainer** is the most commonly used and fits on a variety of tins and glasses. They are usually combined with a Boston shaker. It was named after the bar of the inventor who created it in the late-1800s when the Julep strainer gained popularity but a better model was needed. The Hawthorn strainer is a flat, perforated metal device with a wire coil around the perimeter that neatly traps pulp and ice. It has a short handle with two or four tabs extended from the top and the sides to keep it in place on the shaker.

A **julep strainer** is a perforated metal strainer with slightly inward-curved edges and a functional handle. It was the first purpose-built cocktail strainer. Before the julep strainer, bartenders were using tea strainers. A Julep strainer, instead, was initially used by drinkers to hold back the ice and mint while taking a sip of their drink. Today it is mainly used to strain stirred drinks from a mixing glass.

A **fine-mesh strainer** is used with the Hawthorne strainer in a double strain or fine strain process to prevent micro pieces of fruits and herbs (placed in the shaker) from ending up in the glass. (See page 54 for straining techniques.)

JIGGERS: SINGLE AND DOUBLE

Though they had been around for centuries, jiggers became very useful in the 1800s when cocktails became more complex, helping bartenders portion out the spirits correctly. In 1893 Cornelius P. Dungan invented the double-sided jigger, two different sizes cone-shaped on opposites ends of the same vessel.

Jiggers are the most reliable way to measure liquids, and there are two main types, **single** and **classic double**. The single one (also called a nip or shot glass) is made of a single bowl measuring 1½ ounces (45 ml) in most cases (every country has its own legislation about alcohol measuring). Dungan's jigger (a.k.a. the classic double) is still the most common: usually made of metal and hourglass-shaped, one cone holds 1 ounce (30 ml), called a pony shot, and the other one 1½ ounces (45 ml), called a fluid jigger or jigger shot. Nowadays, they come in various sizes, so you can commonly find 1 ounce on one side and 2 ounces (60 ml) on the other side.

Other types of jiggers are the **Japanese** and the **Bell**. The first is a double jigger with a slim design, taller and smaller diameter rims, making it easy to pour a cocktail with less spilling. It often comes with marks inside, offering a few different liquid measurements. A Bell jigger is a double jigger with a slight weight and a wide rim, which helps to avoid overpouring and overflowing.

THE VAST WORLD OF OPENERS

Whether you are a professional bartender or an enthusiast who wants to build a home bar, always remember to have a bottle opener with you. It allows you to open bottles and mixers quickly. There is a wide range of styles. The **crown cork opener** is the original bottle opener. It is made of a metal piece with a rectangular or rounded opening in one end and a large, solid handle on the other. A **bar blade** (or speed blade) is a 7-inch (17-centimeter) long thin blade with a hole in each end. If you go deep into this world, you can find many others, such as the one attached to the wall (wall-mounted) or the multi-opener, made of various openers.

The same goes for the wine world; there are various styles of openers. A **classic corkscrew** extracts corks easily without crumbling or damaging them. It is made of a single screw that rotated down into the cork, and it pulls it out. If it has two arms, it is called a **winged corkscrew**; if it has two blades, it is called an **Ah-So cork puller**; and if it has a penknife shape, it is called a **waiter's corkscrew** or server's corkscrew. So, you have plenty of choices. You just need to decide which one you prefer.

That is basically all the essential equipment you need for making a home bar or starting a bartender career. Now, let's get into all the other tools that make the job easier and let you prepare a wide range of cocktails. And, of course, some of these are just fancy!

BARSPOON

The barspoon evolved from the old eating utensil used by many cultures around the world. The first evolution was called a Sucket Spoon and had a spoon on one end and a fork on the other to help pick fruit from the syrups of a German dessert. In France, instead, a Mazagran spoon had a flat muddling head (opposite to a bowl end) to help crush medicines into a powder or the hard sugar used in the mazagran, a popular coffee-based drink.

Generally speaking, a barspoon is made with metal with a shallow bowl and a long, spiral handle that helps pour the drink, allowing it to create a layered cocktail (see page 57 for layering technique) without getting stuck in between ice cubes. But we can categorize them as an **American barspoon**, which measures one standard teaspoon, has a twisted handlebar spoon with a small plastic red cap opposite to the bowl end; and a **European barspoon**, which has a twisted handle with a muddler opposite a flat bowl end, and it measures 0.08 ounce (2.5 ml) of liquid. A **Japanese barspoon** has a twisted handle and a weight teardrop shape opposite to the bowl. Sometimes it can be found with a small fork for picking out garnishes.

Barspoons are useful for stirring, muddling, and measuring. Since they are longer than regular spoons, they fit in any glassware. When you choose a barspoon, go for a heavier one because it will be easier to stir. A barspoon should also be long enough (12–15 inches, or 30–38 centimeters) for you to be comfortable while stirring without hitting the vessel's rim.

CUTTING BOARD AND KNIVES

If you want your cocktails to look beautiful, you need to cut your garnish on a **cutting board** with a proper knife. Having a cutting board allows you to make your drinks safely and cleanly. Wood cutting boards are suitable for knives, and they last longer. Other types of good boards are made from polyethylene or polypropylene; try to avoid smooth plastic because the blades tend to slip or the glass board because it makes the knife dull. Then, mind the measure and do not use a too small board; otherwise, the fruits you are cutting will just fall on the countertop.

As for **knives**, the choice may depend on different variants. A bartender's knife needs to be small and light to get delicate garnishes. Ideally, the length of the blade, which should be double-edged, should be around 5 inches (12 centimeters) so that you will be able to cut a pineapple but at the same time carve citrus zest. Knives are made with stainless steel, carbon, or ceramic. Stainless steel is the most common and more practical. Carbon steels are more beautiful and preferred by Japanese bartenders. When honed, they can be sharper than stainless steel, but they require more careful cleaning. Ceramic knives are easy to wash and very sharp, but they are quite delicate and can't be used for cutting hard items, such as a cinnamon stick.

Japanese knives are my favorite. Beautifully designed, the blades are thin and delicate to allow a precise cut and elegant presentation.

MUDDLER

Muddlers are needed for that category of cocktails where fresh herbs require releasing their aroma without being bruised, such as a Mojito. Muddlers help to process the herbs into a paste, and integrate granulated or cubed sugar into cocktails. They evolved from the toddy stick (a multi-purpose tool used in the bars in the eighteen century) and adapted to modern cocktails. They come in a variety of materials and sizes. The head can be flat or toothed. The flat ones are slower and more precise and avoid over-muddling. Toothed heads are more effective in crushing and extracting juice from fruit, but they quickly over-muddle herbs if not used carefully. They are about six to eight inches long (15-20 cm) and about one inch (2.5 cm) in diameter. In general, they are made of wood, plastic, or stainless steel. The wood one is the most popular and durable, but they require more attention in cleaning maintenance. Plastic muddlers are suitable for a juicer, while stainless steel is less breakable and can crush hard ingredients, such as nuts and spices. (See page 56 for muddling techniques.)

Y PEELERS, GRATERS, AND ZESTERS

The **Y peeler** (named after its shape) is a sharp, stainless steel blade that removes fruit and vegetable skins and turns them into gorgeous garnishes.

A **grater** makes very thin shavings of the product you use against it. Chocolate, oranges, and spices' flavors will be quickly and effectively extracted.

A **zester** is a tool to create twisted zest and infuse the drink with the fruit's oils. The most used is the channel knife, a small knife with a V-shaped metal blade at the end of the handle, surrounded by a rectangle frame. These knives are used to cut strips of citrus fruits, cucumbers, and other vegetables to get a spiral shape for the twist of a garnish or create different design shapes, like a flower one.

JUICERS

Whether it is a **citrus reamer**, a **hand juicer**, or an **electric model**, this tool can save your life when you need to squeeze citrus for a cocktails party. Plus, freshly squeezed juice makes a big difference in the taste and quality of the cocktails. The first known juicer came from Turkey (Kütahya, precisely), back in the eighteenth century, and it was used to make a citrus drink. By the end of the nineteenth century, it reached the United States, where different models were invented and patented. Nowadays, it is found in any kitchen (professional or at home), and it can be manual or electric. The manual ones are glass or plastic reamers (a.k.a. a **countertop citrus reamer**) with a pointed cone, surrounded by a well that collects the juice, and nubbles meant to stop the seeds from falling into the juice. The fruit is simply pressed onto the cone to extract the juice. A **handheld citrus reamer** is just a blade mounted on a rounded handle, and it is very easy to use. A **citrus squeezer** has a levered construction with a hinged bowl and handles that need to be pushed to extract the juice. **Manual press juicers** are great when you need to squeeze a large quantity of juice. The fruit is placed on top of a perforated cone, where it is pushed into it by a metal cap pulled down by a lever.

There are various electric juicers on the market. A masticating juicer (a.k.a. a **cold press juicer** or **slow juicer**) uses a slow rotating auger and a screen to crush and press out the juice. A **centrifugal juicer** spins with spinning blades against a mesh filter, separating the juice from the body and then separating the juice from the pulp. A **triturating juicer** (a.k.a. a twin-gear juicer) has two gears that rotate to crush and grind the ingredient into tiny particles to extract the juice, pushing out the dry pulp. Finally, a **steam juicer** is a stack of nesting pots and a tube to pour off the juice from fruits and vegetables. It extracts the juice by warming the ingredients and separating the juice from the pulp.

MIXING GLASS: PINT AND YARAI

Once you know that you can use any glass (or even a metal shaker's tin, or other vessel) to stir your cocktails, a mixing glass is one of the beautiful tools that makes your life easy. In fact, a mixing glass allows you to control the texture, dilution, and clarity of the cocktail.

The most common mixing glass is the **pint glass** which holds sixteen ounces (470 ml). It is tapered toward the base, and it is typically the large tin of the Boston shaker.

A **Yarai glass** is a Japanese product named after the Japanese diamond pattern engraved on the outside. It is a thicker beaker-shaped glass with straight sides, a heavy base, and a spout that make it easy to pour the cocktail. It is sturdy and holds a chill longer. The wide base allows a faster and smoother stirring, and the wide mouth avoids splashes out of the glass.

POUR SPOUTS

Invented by John J. Daly in 1963, the first pourer was made of plastic and was a free flow prototype. Also called liquor pourers, speed pourers, or bottle pourers, pour spouts are essentials behind the bar and fancy tools in your home bar. They help manage the flow of a bottle's pour and, while free pouring, you can do it rapidly and accurately, avoiding over-pouring, spillage, and time-wasting. There are many pourers on the market. Let us see the main ones.

A standard **metal pourer** (or free-flow pourer) is commonly used, and it usually features a rubber seal. With a standard pourer, the liquid flows smoothly and quickly.

A **tapered pourer** (or angled pourer) has a long, slim spout that makes the pour quick and precise, allowing consistent and high-flow rate pours.

A **screened pourer** has a tiny screen inside, preventing any insect from falling into the bottle. This pourer has a low-flow rate because of the screen, making it difficult to pour creamy spirits or syrups. Similar are Flap pourers with a built-in flap that keeps insects out and does not affect the pour speed. Some of them open automatically when the bottle is tilted; others need to be opened manually. Even in this case, thicker spirits can get stuck on the flap.

Ball pourers (or measured pourers) are designed to allow pours of 1 ounce to 1½ ounces (45 ml), keeping strict control over the use of spirits and reducing costs. This pourer opens to allow the alcohol to pass through and then shut off to prevent overpouring.

BLENDER

Blenders are useful for crushing ice, preparing puree fruit, and making frozen cocktails. There are different types of blenders, but large capacity is usually preferred. Also, speed and motor power count. If the blender has a good amount of speed options, you will have more control over the drink's consistency. When purchasing a blender, mind the motor power. If you go for a low-watt blender, the risk that it will break soon is high. Plus, if you want to crush the ice, only a high-watt blender will do (500 watts or more). The lid's seal needs to be good and thigh; otherwise, you will end up with chunks of fruits everywhere. Finally, go for a glass or stainless steel pitcher with stainless steel blades because they are more durable than the plastic one.

ICE TOOLS

Ice is one of the most important ingredients when making cocktails. It cools down the drink and dilutes the alcohol. According to its shape and size, it will have different dilution times, preserving the flavor of the spirits and the cocktail itself.

Ice cube trays: unless you want to buy a bag of ice each time you make drinks, go for an ice cube tray. (Store-bought ice may seem the quickest, but in the end, it will cost more than buying a couple of cube trays.) Small ice cubes (which are generally sold in the bags) break down easily and dilute too fast, but if you buy a silicone tray that holds large cubes, then you will have a problem less. In fact, the problem you could have with the tray is that the ice in the freezer tends to absorb food odors, so if you can find a lid, you will solve this problem too, and you will maintain the integrity of the ice as well. A block of ice (that you can cut and carve to fit the glass) is the best choice among these three home methods. In fact, on a block of ice, there is less surface than on multiple smaller cubes, meaning it will melt slower, reducing the dilution time too. In any of these cases, though, the ice will be cloudy because of the impurities and trapped air retained during the freezing process. Cloudy ice will melt faster than clear ice due to less density. So, clear ice is the preferred option (not only for aesthetic reasons).

Then, if you think about the right type of ice for a specific drink, you will not get out quickly from this labyrinth, mainly because the biggest ice is not always the correct choice. Generally speaking, a standard ice cube is suitable for shaking and stirring and for highball cocktails or old-fashioneds. A large ice cube or block of ice is good for shaking because it improves the drink's texture and helps to aerate it. Crushed ice is used to soften the ingredients' intensity and give an immediate chilling effect to the drink. That is why it is used with spirit-forward cocktails that need dilution.

Ice bucket: in a restaurant, they are a must. They keep wine and champagne chilled. You can use them for the same reason at home but try to avoid using them to keep the ice. It is always better to grab directly from the freezer the right quantity of ice you need to make your cocktail at home. This is because when ice stays outside the freezer for too long, it will release a bunch of water straight away when added to the drink. So good for chilling your wine, but not to keep your ice.

Lewis bag: it is a sturdy canvas bag, with a tie, filled with ice cubes and then beaten with a wooden mallet to get crushed ice. Since it is sturdy, the canvas will not break or leak. The ice chips won't shoot out because the canvas will be sealed. The Lewis bag was the traditional way to crush ice in the nineteenth century.

Ice pick and ice pick chipper: both are essential tools if you want to dig into the cutting ice process. The ice pick has a single rigid point on a wooden handle, and it is used to separate or break up small cubes of ice. An ice pick chipper has, traditionally, a wooden handle with five flattened nail-shaped prongs. Today, they more commonly have six rounded shape prongs, and it is about nine inches (2.5 cm) long. It can easily break up a block of ice and separate chunks of ice.

Ice tapper: a vintage tool for truly passionate. It was popular in the 1950s, and it was used to break smaller pieces of ice. It is a flexible plastic stick with a stainless steel ball in one hand.

Ice scoops and tongs: the first makes it faster to fill a glass with ice, while ice tongs allow you to pick only one cube per time. If behind a professional bar, they are a request by health and safety procedure (in most countries, it is a legal requirement to use them); they are a nice touch to add to your set at your home bar. Tongs can be used not only for picking ice but for fruit and garnishes as well.

Ice knife: generally, any good, serrated knife will do the job, but if you want to use something more professional, go for the Japanese ice saw, a specialized blade with an easy-to-grip-shaped handle.

Clear ice maker: as mentioned before, clear ice is better than cloudy ice. It is beautiful, melts slowly, and contains fewer impurities compared to cloudy ice. On the market, a few brands are selling clear ice makers (or molds too). They all use the same process, directional freezing: controlling the direction in which the fluids solidifies can affect the final result. So, if the liquid thickens from one side only, the impurities and air bubbles will be pushed in one direction, creating a pure, clear, uniform structure. The clear ice maker on the market circulates the water over a freezing cold grid, so that ice freezes from the inside out or one layer at a time. The purest water freezes while the impurities move along. If you don't want to spend too much money, but you are still interested in getting better and clear ice, here's a trick that will get you the same result. Get an insulated cooler that can fit your freezer, filling it with water (no need to be distilled or boiled), and place it into the freezer without cover. After one or two days, extract the container and place it in the sink. Let it rest for fifteen minutes and then turn it upside down and carefully remove the block (if it doesn't, gently hammer along sides to release it). If you remove the cooler when you notice that the water at the bottom is not entirely solid, it will be easier to remove the block from the cooler. Then, with a knife or the ice tools described above, cut the ice as you preferred (keep in mind what kind of cocktail you are going to make).

SOUS VIDE

Sous vide (which means under vacuum in French) is a cooking technique that enables you to prepare food with more tenderness and flavor at a precise temperature in a water bath.

Sealed-cooking practices appeared in the Middle Ages when it was common to use animal organs to prepare food. But it was only in the late 1700s that the concept of low and slow cooking was described by Benjamin Thompson, who discovered that he could cook the potatoes using only low-temperature hot air. The research continued only in the 1960s when American and French engineers found that food had improved flavors and textures with this method and developed an industrial food preservation method. Georges Pralus adopted the technique in 1974 for the Restaurant Troisgros. Another pioneer was Bruno Goussault, who created guidelines for cooking times and temperatures.

In sous vide, food or liquids are vacuum-sealed and slow-cooked in the water at a constant low temperature. In the bartending world, it is a new technique, and it can be used for making syrups, cordials, and dense ingredients, such as cinnamon bark and dried species. For this technique, you just need to attach a precision cooker to a pot of water and set the time and temperature according to your desired level (or the one indicated for a specific ingredient), sealed the food or liquid into a bag, and clip it to the inside of the pot.

SIPHON: WHIPPED CREAM AND SODA

A siphon is made of a canister in which ingredients are poured, a head fixed on the canister and where chargers are screwed, a spout that can be of various sizes and shapes, and a charger.

There are two types of siphon: whipped cream and soda. The difference is in the head. Holding the siphon up (head up), in the soda one, the spout points down, while in the cream one, the spout points up. Both can be made of aluminum or stainless steel. A cream charger contains N_2O, meaning two atoms of nitrogen (N) and one of oxygen (O). Soda charger is, instead, made of CO_2 (carbon dioxide).

Whipped cream siphons are great to make beautiful and tasty foam on top of your drinks. You can make foam from water, white egg, and nitrous oxide (N_2O), but you can easily change the liquid part with tea, juice, or any other liquid that is not oily and provides an alcohol content under 20%. As a substitute for egg white, you can use gelatin or agar-agar. If you are looking for a sweet foam, add sugar syrup, honey, or agave syrup to amplify the foam's flavor.

A **soda siphon** is used to carbonate water but can be used for a cocktail, too (be sure that the one you purchased can carbonate liquids other than water). Carbonation creates a more rounded flavor, and the colder the siphon is, the more carbonated the cocktail will be.

To use the siphon (either with the cream charger or the soda one), combine the ingredients you chose into the siphon base without overfilling (read the instructions, but generally, you need to fill it to half capacity). Before this process, carefully remove any pulp or solids that can clog the siphon and, again, make sure that you can insert liquids other than water in the soda siphon. This is really important because you can put yourself in jeopardy. Plus, overfilling may lead to the explosion of the tool, so carefully read the instruction. Screw-in the head and firmly onto the canister. Place the charger into the holder with the smallest end facing down. Twist the charger holder onto the head of the canister until the gas starts to be released. Shake the dispenser a few times and place it in the fridge for a couple of hours. Then turn it upside down and press the lever to release the foam or soda water.

Be aware of the potentials dangers of mixing nitrous oxide and high pressure inside a charger.

TECHNIQUES: FROM THE BASIC TO THE ADVANCED LEVEL

Once you have your new tools, the spirits you like, and a bunch of ingredients that you want to use to make a cocktail, you are missing only one thing: mixing techniques. Some of them are easy to learn, others require some time to master. But eventually, with time, effort and study, you will perfect them. Mastering these techniques (if you haven't already) will make you feel more confident and comfortable both behind a bar and in front of your friends. Do not be afraid of experimenting, trying, playing. After all, only practicing will improve your skills and make the perfect cocktail.

Pouring

Pouring can be done through a jigger, or it can be free pouring directly into the glass or shaker. With a jigger, you will be more accurate, and the cocktail will be more balanced, even if it takes more time. Free pouring allows you to be quicker because you can pour multiple bottles at once, but even the slightest mistake will affect the cocktail's quality and taste. Nowadays, plenty of bartending schools teach how to master the free pour techniques to measure the pours down to the millimeter accurately. Of course, it takes time to get to this level, but training and practicing will help achieve the result.

Straining

The straining technique removes any solid parts from the final cocktail, such as ice or pulp (single straining). It is one of the most used bartending skills, and it is one of the last processes to do before garnishing a cocktail. A double straining removes larger objects, making the cocktail smoother, and it is commonly used with shaken drinks. If you are not using a built-in strainer shaker, then you may use three different strainers (see page 42).

To use a Hawthorne strainer, just place it over a Boston shaker (or a French one), push down the tabs to keep it in place and solely pour the cocktail into your glass.

To use a julep strainer, just hold it firmly and ensure that it is touching the side of the glass from where the liquid is poured from, so that it will not slip. The cupped face needs to be faced down while the flat side needs to face out of the glass (that is the traditional way).

To use a fine-mesh strainer (for a double straining), after placing the Hawthorne strainer on the top of the shaker, hold the fine-mesh strainer between the shaker/strainer and the glass. Slowly pour the cocktail through the Hawthorne strainer, then the fine-mesh strainer, and finally, into the glass.

Stirring

Stirring requires precision, and it is used to chill and gently combine the ingredients of a cocktail to create a smooth texture without incorporating air. It is a technique to use with spirit-only cocktails, and it requires a barspoon and a mixing glass or a shaker.

To stir, fill your vessels with ice, combine your ingredients, and insert a bar spoon into it. Hold the stem between your thumb and first two fingers, then twirl the spoon back and forth around the perimeter of the vessel in continuous and consistent motion. Try to keep the bar spoon in constant contact with the vessel's inside and move the ice in a steady, circular motion. Once the vessel is icy cold (it takes approximately 17–20 seconds), remove the spoon and strain the liquid into a chilled glass.

Shaking

The shaking method allows chilling and mixing ingredients, infusing them with air and aerating them so that the drink's texture changes, becoming lighter.

There are three classic shaking techniques.

A **wet shake** is when the drink is shaken with ice. A **dry shake** is with no ice and used mainly for frothing ingredients, such as egg whites, and typically followed by a wet shake. The third type of technique (which I don't recommend) is the **reverse dry shake**, meaning a wet shake, followed by a dry shake. A reverse dry shake can result in plenty of foam, but with bigger bubbles and less creaminess; often, the cocktail is watered down and has lost its chill.

When shaking, you need to consider a couple of factors: a cocktail needs to be shaken for ten to fifteen seconds (if less, it won't be cold enough; if more, it will be over diluted), the shake needs to be hard and fast.

When you shake, measure your ingredients and combine them into the large tin, fill three-fourths full of ice, and add the metal part on the top (Boston shaker, page 41) or put on the cobbler shaker cap (cobbler shaker, page 41) and seal it firmly with a good tap. The ice will do the rest: it will chill the stainless steel tin, forming a nice tight seal. Shake for 12–15 seconds (if you are a beginner, hold both parts to have more control). The classic method to hold a shaker is to place your thumbs on both tins' base with the pinkies intertwined in the middle. To be fair, you should hold the shaker how you are comfortable without forgetting important steps. If you are using a Boston with a metal tin and a glass one, always remember to keep the metal part on the bottom when you open it because the glass tin sometimes causes spillage when hitting. Ensure that the ice is hitting both ends of the shaker. To open the shaker: in a Boston shaker, hold it with one hand and with the other firmly tap the lip of the tin (the point where the tin and the glass meet). You will get used to it, don't worry. It sounds more complicated than it actually is. With a cobbler shaker, just remove the cap. Finally, strain the mixture into a cocktail glass.

To Shake or Not to Shake? That is the Question

A general rule of thumb is that if the cocktail is only spirits-made, you need to stir it, because you want to maintain the right flavor profile and not want to over dilute and over chill it. If the cocktail's ingredients include fruit juice, dairy products, eggs, or creamy spirits, you need to shake. The reason is quite clear: stirring only spirits is easier than trying to stir a spirit with heavy cream, for example. It is easier and better to shake hard ingredients to combine them.

Churning

Churning is the technique you use to stir a drink with crushed ice to chill it quickly. You need to churn in the glass you want to use, using a barspoon. Stir up and down, back and forth, to mix all the layers of the cocktail.

Building

Building means constructing a cocktail right inside the glass you are going to serve it in. It is a very easy method since you simply need to fill the vessel with ice and pour in the ingredients one after the other. It is used mainly for simple recipes with few ingredients.

Muddling

Muddling is a practice that allows you to crush an ingredient to extract and release its flavor. It is commonly used with fresh ingredients, such as herbs and citrus fruits. It looks like an easy method, but bitterness can come up and unbalance the drink if you over-muddle some elements.

To muddle ingredients together, use a muddler (see page 46) to crush a component directly into the glass you will serve the drink in. This can be done in a rocks glass when serving an old-fashioned, for example. But if the glass is not sturdy enough to withstand the muddling force, then do this technique in a mixing glass. Push down and crush the ingredients until you extract their juices and oils.

Throwing

This technique is used to thicken liquid ingredients when stirring wouldn't mix them properly and shaking would break up the drink's viscosity. Throwing allows you to create air bubbles (tinier than those obtained from a good shake) and give a natural texture to the cocktail.

To throw a drink, you need two vessels, generally the two tins of a shaker. Fill one tin two-thirds full of ice and add ingredients, and place a strainer on top to allow the liquid to be poured but not the ice. Then pour the drink back and forth between the two vessels, increasing the distance between them so that you end up pouring from a height.

Rolling

Instead of the horizontal back and forth moving shake, the rolling is a gentle way to mix a cocktail between the hands. It still allows to mix the ingredients and chill the cocktail.

To roll a cocktail, fill a tin with ice and combine the ingredients. Then move ("roll") the shaker vertically in a circular motion.

Layering

The layering technique is when you gently and slowly pour the different liquids over a barspoon (see page 44) so that one falls onto the other and rests atop in a new layer. To do this, you should know the density of the liquids you are using. Sometimes it can be not easy, especially when a liquid is made by different producers who can alternate the formula and, therefore, the density. Some other liquids are fairly simple to understand their texture. The rule to follow is heavy liquids, such as crème de cacao or any other creamy spirits, go first, while lighter liquids, such as triple sec or vodka, will usually float on top of any heavier liquid. As a general rule thumb, heavy spirits have more sugar, while lighter spirits have more alcohol.

Blending

Blending incorporates ice into a cocktail, making it smoother and colder than any other technique. Mainly used for frozen drinks, you can also mix heavier ingredients to achieve a thicker texture.

You simply need a blender, the ingredients, and ice (if you need to make a frozen cocktail). The ice has to be more than liquids (almost double of the liquid parts): too much ice means the drink will be chunky, and you will need to wait until it melts; also, less ice means the drink will melt too quickly. So always keep in mind the consistency to make a perfect frozen drink.

Flaming

Be very careful when you use this technique. Many liqueurs are highly flammable; therefore, flaming is hazardous and needs to be performed under cautious circumstances. Do not let a drink burn too long; otherwise, it may explode, and do not blow it out. Do not pour high-proof alcohol onto an already flaming drink, and never drink a cocktail that is still on fire.

Having said that, flaming is used to enhance the flavor of cocktails by setting it alight. There are two methods for flaming a drink.

The first one is touching the surface of the drink with a lighted match until it catches fire. Let it burn for ten seconds and then extinguish it with a small saucer on top of the glass. If the drink is flamed for too long, do not drink it straight away because the glass, as well as the cocktail, will be scorching.

The second and most common technique is citrus flaming. When alight, citrus peel caramelizes and gives a smoky aroma to the cocktail. To do so, light a match (not a lighter) and hold it on top of the cocktail; with the other hand, grab a citrus peel and hold it close to the flame. Squeeze it to release the oils through the flame and onto the drink. Extinguish the flame and discard the citrus peel.

Blue Blazer

Created in 1862 by Jerry Thomas, a blue blazer is when you throw flaming alcohol from one vessel to another. It is a very difficult technique to learn, and the same cautions applied to the flaming technique must be applied to this one. Use common sense and stay safe.

To do a blue blazer, combine a spirit (usually whiskey), hot water, and other ingredients (typically sugar, a syrup, and bitters) in a heat-resistant (preferably silver-plated) mug with a handle. With a blowtorch, heat the filled mug and do the same with a second mug. Then light the mix on fire and throw it from one mug to another about five times. Start with the mugs close and then increase the distance. If done correctly, you will see a considerable stream of blue fire going back and forth between the vessels. Pour the drink into a thick glass (one that can handle the heat) and cover it with one mug to extinguish the flames.

Before attempting a blue blazer, it is good to practice using water instead of an already flaming spirit.

Chilling

It is not a technique, per se, but an important practice when making cocktails is chilling your glassware, because your cocktails will remain cooler for longer. There are two ways to chill a glass.

Either you can store the glassware into the fridge or freezer or fill the glass with ice, let it sits for a couple of minutes, and then discard the ice before pouring the cocktail. If adequately chilled, the glassware should be frosted outside.

GARNISHES

As the final touch that gives a pleasant aspect to the cocktail, garnishes have become very important. They are appealing, but they can also add flavor to the cocktail's profile, show your attention to detail (especially if you are making the drink for your friends), and elevate the presentation.

In the past few years, recent garnishes trends have acquired fame in the bartending industry, and they can be divided into the following. **Vintage** where, as in the past, the garnish is an ingredient of the cocktail that, instead of being wasted, could be reused; **tiki** is the one that uses the flamboyant flower to garnish the cocktails; **modern** is about a variety of things, from dried flowers to gold leaf; **culinary** is the one that has approached the food world and has experimented with it.

In any of these scenarios, a few aspects need to be taken into consideration. The garnish's freshness and high quality: if it is not fresh, the drink will be better off. Freshness and high quality can make the difference, so always keep the garnish well maintained (for example, mint needs to be wrapped in a damp paper towel and stored in the fridge). Sharpen your cutting skills to get lovely garnishes as well. Get a knife, a cutting board, and the ingredient you want to transform into a garnish. Just keep focus and try until you get what you pictured in your mind. It is not a difficult task, but it takes time to cut elegantly.

Garnishes can be edible and not edible. The first category includes citrus, fruits, herbs, spices, and savory. **Citrus** is the most common garnish and can be used in various ways. We have wedges: just wash the citrus, chop off the heads, cut in half, remove the pit, and slice in wedges. Rule of thumb: a lime can be cut in six wedges, a lemon in eight, and orange in sixteen. Twists require a channel knife (see page 46) to go around the fruit in a spiral, starting from where the stem was. Remember that it needs to be long enough to curl it. The wider it is, the looser the curl will be. To make a coin, just cut a thin round peel, about 1 inch (2.5 centimeters). You use it as a garnish, to squeeze the oil over the glass or to flame it. For making wheels, remove the head of the fruit, make a deep cut to reach the inner pulp, and slice off quarter-inch wheels. Both with a whole wheel and a half wheel, cut a slit in the center to hang it onto the rim of the glass. Dehydrated citrus has a bitter taste and has a longer shelf life. Cut the citrus into slices and heat them in the oven (each ingredient has its own warming time).

Besides citrus, other **fruits** can be used. Cherries, both fresh and Maraschino types, are quite popular. You can just sit one into the glass or hang a few of them on a stick. Another example is the pineapple, often used on the rim of a glass.

Herbs and **spices** offer a pungent taste. Mint spring is one of the most used garnish, especially in summer drinks. Herbs, in general, bring a nice flavor to the cocktail, refreshing it. On the other side, species, such as cinnamon and nutmeg, give a warm taste to the drink. Savory garnish, such as olive and almonds, are also more than welcomed.

A **rim** is a garnish too. This technique consists of covering the rim of the glassware with a dry ingredient. The most used ones are salt and sugar. The first rule to make a good rim is that the ingredient must stay outside of the glass. If it goes inside, when you pour your cocktail, it will be like adding an extra ingredient that you actually do not want, and that will affect the drink's final flavor.

To rim a glass, take a lime or a lemon wedge and pass the pulp over the glass's rim until the whole perimeter is moist. Grab the glass from the base or the stem and, upside down, let it rest in a shallow saucer where you put your dry ingredient. Rotate the glass until the whole rim is coated. Instead of using a citrus wedge, you can wet the rim with one ingredient of the cocktail, such a spirit.

Finally, we have a wide range of **non-edible garnishes**. They are not used to enhance the cocktails' flavor but amaze the guests (if in a restaurant or a cocktail bar) or friends (at your home bar). The non-edible garnishes set your imagination and creativity free.

CHAPTER 1:
BRUNCH AND LUNCH
COCKTAILS

It is a Sunday morning; you went to sleep late the night before, maybe you had one drink too many, so you wake up late. You are hungry, terribly hungry. But it is 10.30, and you can't just have a cup of coffee or a cup of milk with cereals. It is too late. You think. Maybe you can cook, but still, it is 10:30 a.m. You can't cook a Sunday roast; it is too early. Then you have a great idea. Brunch!

Brunch is famously the meal that happens when it is too late to be called breakfast but too early to be named lunch. That is why it is a combination of the two words.

It has its roots in England, at the end of the nineteenth century, when the wealthy British upper classes would give their servants a day off, after preparing a buffet meal that the families could eat from throughout the entire day. Sitting around a banquet table, they enjoyed the multi-course meal and drank the finest alcohol while chatting over the past week's events.

Nowadays, brunch mostly happens on the weekend from 10:00 a.m. to 2:00 p.m., but it can go on until 5:00 p.m., depending on the city. A typical brunch includes savory dishes and sweet ones, so here they come, eggs Benedict, followed by pancakes covered in maple syrup, all accompanied by fizzy cocktails that will brighten your day—and your mood!

A CLOUDY MANDARIN

Tasting notes: fruity, sweet, creamy

With fresh and fruity notes of orange and mandarin, and the complexity of coffee and cardamom with a creamy finish, this is a smooth, clean session drink to start your brunch with. You won't notice how strong it is; it goes down like water. Your guests will love it!

YIELD: 1 COCKTAIL

1⅓ ounces (40 ml) Coffee Bean-Infused Mezcal (page 198)

⅓ ounce (10 ml) orange liqueur, such as Cointreau

⅔ ounce (20 ml) fino sherry

1 teaspoon (5 ml) Maraschino Luxardo

2 drops cardamom tincture (page 245)

Top up with Mandarin Foam (page 181)

(1) Fill a mixing glass or a metal shaking tin with ice.

(2) Pour coffee bean-infused mezcal, orange liqueur, fino sherry, Maraschino Luxardo, and cardamom tincture into the chilled vessel, and stir rapidly with a bar spoon for 17 to 20 seconds.

(3) Strain into a chilled highball glass over ice.

(4) Top up with mandarin foam.

Bartender's Tip: *Pair this cocktail with the delicate flavor of roasted chicken or pumpkin ravioli. If you crave something sweet, then match it with a chocolate mousse.*

BERRYKILLA JULEP

Tasting notes: light, fizzy, sweet

Berrykilla Julep is a minty, delightful, tequila-based drink that incorporates the spiced flavor of Amaro Montenegro. Champagne makes the drink light and perfect to have during your brunch or lunch, almost like eating a raspberry jam croissant! The mint leaves give it a long, pleasant aftertaste.

YIELD: 1 COCKTAIL

---

1 ounce (30 ml) tequila

½ ounce (15 ml) Amaro Montenegro

1⅓ ounces (40 ml) champagne

½ ounce (15 ml) Raspberry Syrup (page 240)

⅓ ounce (10 ml) freshly squeezed lime juice

6 mint leaves

2 or 3 raspberries

2 mint springs

Confectioner's sugar

(1) Combine tequila, Amaro Montenegro, champagne, raspberry syrup, lime juice, and mint leaves in a julep cup.

(2) Fill half of the cup with crushed ice, and with a bar spoon, gently press the mint leaves and stir for 6 seconds.

(3) Add some more crushed ice to the top of the cup.

(4) Garnish with raspberries, mint springs, and confectioner's sugar on top of the mint.

APPLELIZA

Tasting notes: light, smoky, fruity

The Appleliza is the perfect, summery cocktail to drink poolside. It is a concoction of mezcal, lime and apple juices, Amaro Montenegro, and Cucumber Cordial. It is so refreshing and good that you will lose count of how many of them you have had! Here it is, your new troublemaker.

YIELD: 1 COCKTAIL

1⅓ ounce (40 ml) mezcal, preferably Vida Del Maguey

⅓ ounce (10 ml) fresh-squeezed lime juice

2⅓ ounce (70 ml) apple juice

⅔ ounce (20 ml) Amaro Montenegro

⅓ ounce (10 ml) Cucumber Cordial (page 188)

1 slice cucumber

(1) Pour mezcal, lime juice, apple juice, Amaro Montenegro, and cucumber cordial into a chilled highball glass filled with ice.

(2) Gently stir until chilled.

(3) Garnish with a slice of cucumber on a skewer.

Bartender's Tip: *The Appleliza is a perfect brunch cocktail because it is light, fruity, and refreshing. Vida Del Maguey is the best choice for Appleliza because it is a quite fruity and spiced mezcal itself and it lights up Amaro Montenegro beautifully. If you do not like it or cannot find it, then go for another fruity mezcal, such as Real Minero Barril Artesanal. And remember, the Appleliza is versatile; you can substitute apple juice with another summer fruit juice, such as watermelon juice.*

CALL YOUR MAMA

Tasting notes: spicy, savory, smoky

Could you ever brunch without a Bloody Mary? Nope, so here it is, my twist! Call Your Mama is the right drink when you need a warm and comforting hug after a long night. Maybe you had a drink too many; maybe you just drank the wrong cocktails. And now, what you need is an intense, delicious cocktail that will make you feel like you are reborn. Call Your Mama is smokier and stronger than a classic Bloody Mary or Bloody Maria. If you prefer it less smoky, try this recipe with tequila.

YIELD: 1 COCKTAIL

1⅓ ounces (40 ml) mezcal

⅓ ounce (10 ml) fino sherry

2 teaspoons (10 ml) Worcestershire sauce

2⅓ ounces (70 ml) tomato juice

2 teaspoons (10 ml) pickled juice

⅔ ounce (20 ml) freshly squeezed lemon juice

⅓ ounce (10 ml) Simple Syrup 2:1 (page 242)

1 pinch black pepper

4 dashes hot sauce*

2 cornichons

Pinch of salt (to season the cornichon)

1 lime wedge

1 Parmesan Chip (page 183)

*Four drops hot sauce generally make the drink medium spicy. If you like it very hot, add up to ten drops.

(1) Fill a metal shaking tin with ice, mezcal, fino sherry, Worcestershire sauce, tomato juice, pickled juice, lemon juice, simple syrup 2:1, black pepper, and hot sauce.

(2) Throw the liquid between the large and the small tin of the shakers 4 or 5 times to give aeration to the cocktail.

(3) Fill a highball with ice and pour the cocktail.

(4) Garnish with cornichon, lime wedge, and a parmesan chip.

FRUITY NEST

Tasting notes: smoked, fruity, tropical

A delightfully fruity and very refreshing long drink, the Fruity Nest is made for those who love sweet and fruity cocktails. It is amazingly easy to drink, and it feels like having summer in your highball. Very versatile, you can also try it as a mocktail. Just add a splash of soda (instead of mezcal), and your kids will love it.

YIELD: 1 COCKTAIL (10 COCKTAILS FOR THE LIQUID IN THE SIPHON)

1¼ cups (300 ml) lychee water*

¾ cup or 6⅔ ounces (200 ml) freshly squeezed lemon juice, from about 5 or 6 lemons

¾ cup (150 ml) Grilled Pineapple Syrup (page 231)

2 ounces (60 ml) mezcal

1 fresh lychee

*Lychee water can be bought at some grocery stores and online or made at home by pureeing a can of lychee, liquid and all.

(1) Combine lychee water, lemon juice, and grilled pineapple syrup in a jar.

(2) Pour the liquid into a soda siphon and fill it with CO_2. Store it in the fridge for 1 hour before serving cocktails.

(3) Fill a highball with ice.

(4) Pour mezcal into the glass and then top up with the sparkling liquid from the siphon.

(5) Gently stir. Garnish with lychee.

(6) Store the remainder of the juice mixture in the siphon in the fridge for up to 2 weeks or until it is fizzy.

Bartender's Tip: If you cannot find lychee water, just buy a can of lychee in syrup. Blitz the entire contents of the can in a blender at high speed for 2 minutes. Fine strain through a muslin cloth or mesh strainer and squeeze as much liquid as possible. Store in the fridge for up to 2 weeks.

LA MEDICINA DEL JIMADOR

Tasting notes: spiced, fruity, rich

La medicina del Jimador is a concoction of flavors. Made with healthy and good ingredients, it will be your new oasis in the desert. Refreshing, thirst-quenching, and delicious, you can drink it anytime and anywhere. I suggest having it as a kind of boozy, liquid fruity salad; you will not be disappointed!

YIELD: 1 COCKTAIL

1⅔ ounces (50 ml) Lemon, Orange, Pink Grapefruit Peel-Infused Mezcal, preferably made with Mezcal Lo Verás Reposdo (page 234)

1 ounce (30 ml) Honey & Ginger Syrup (page 201)

⅔ ounce (20 ml) freshly squeezed lime juice

3⅓ ounces (100 ml) coconut sparkling water

1 lime wedge

(1) Pour coconut water into the soda siphon and fill it with gas.

(2) Store it in the fridge for 1 hour before serving it.

(3) Fill with ice a chilled highball and pour lemon, orange, pink grapefruit peel-infused mezcal, honey and ginger syrup, and lime juice.

(4) Top up with coconut soda and garnish with a lime wedge.

Bartender's Choice: Go for a mezcal that will enhance each ingredient of this cocktail. Mezcal Lo Verás Reposdo can give an extra kick to La medicina del Jimador starting from its aroma, a delicious grilled coconut hint and an oak spice finish. The mezcal, with its toffee and vanilla notes, is a great pair to the coconut soda and honey and ginger syrup of the cocktail. Plus, you will get a pleasant and long finish from Lo Verás Reposado.

MADRE TIERRA

Tasting notes: herbal, earthy, fruity

With a delightful raspberry and basil hint in your mouth, this is just the type of drink you can't say no to. The freshness of the raspberries is a key to the result. And make sure you don't infuse the green tea for too long; otherwise, it will become bitter. The Madre Tierra (Mother Earth) is quite easy to make; you can't go wrong.

YIELD: 1 COCKTAIL

1⅓ ounces (40 ml) mezcal, such as Madre Mezcal

½ ounce (15 ml) Raspberries Chartreuse (page 206)

⅔ ounce (20 ml) Cocchi Americano

⅓ ounce (10 ml) Basil and Jasmine Tea Syrup (page 219)

1 dash absinthe

Raspberry Tuile (page 184), optional, to garnish

(1) Fill and chill a mixing glass or a metal shaking tin with ice.

(2) Pour mezcal, raspberries Chartreuse, Cocchi Americano, basil and green tea syrup, and absinthe into the vessel and stir rapidly with a bar spoon between 17 to 20 seconds.

(3) Strain into a chilled Nick-and-Nora glass.

(4) Garnish with raspberry tuile, if desired.

Bartender's Choice: *Madre Mezcal has fresh herbs and floral notes, which are enchanting in the presence of Chartreuse. It is a fantastic mezcal to use for this cocktail with a long and earthy finish because it keeps all the different flavors in your mouth. Jose Garcia Morales and his family produce Madre Mezcal in San Dionisio, Oaxaca. It is made with 70% maguey Espadín, and 30% maguey Cuixe (agave Karwinskii) and the distillation is done in the family's aged copper still.*

NAKED TRUTH

Tasting notes: herbal, smoky, boil vegetable

A Naked Truth is not your typical cocktail, but it is a light drink suitable for your Sunday brunches with friends. Inspired by a classic Gibson, this twist is just a bit sweeter thanks to the presence of thyme-infused syrup.

YIELD: 1 COCKTAIL

---

1 ounce (30 ml) mezcal, such as Vida Del Maguey

1 ounce (30 ml) dry vermouth

⅓ ounce (10 ml) store-bought onion brine

2 dashes orange bitters

½ ounce (15 ml) Thyme-Infused Syrup (page 244)

1 thyme sprig

(1) Fill a mixing glass or a metal shaking tin with ice.

(2) Pour mezcal, dry vermouth, onion brine, orange bitters, and thyme-infused syrup into the vessel and stir rapidly with a bar spoon for 17 to 20 seconds.

(3) Strain into a chilled Nick-and-Nora glass.

(4) Garnish with a thyme sprig.

Bartender's Choice: *Vida Del Maguey is the perfect match for this drink because the smoke and the spiciness go very well with the saltiness and the onion brine's tartness, which is flavored with thyme. Together they give birth to a delicate and herbal drink.*

PEACHY BUBBLES

Tasting notes: sparkling, fruity, light

Upgrade of the classic Bellini, Peachy Bubbles is still a low–ABV cocktail, despite the mezcal. It is a lovely sparkling drink with a delicious aroma. You will be inebriated from the sweetness of the peach accompanied by a tropical pineapple touch. Lemon oil, squeezed on the top, closes a balanced cocktail.

YIELD: 1 COCKTAIL

¾ ounce (25 ml) mezcal, such as Ilegal Reposado

1⅔ ounces (50 ml) peach puree*

⅓ ounce (10 ml) pineapple juice

1 teaspoon (5 ml) Simple Syrup 2:1 (page 242)

1 ounce (30 ml) prosecco, plus more to top up

1 lemon coin, to squeeze and discard

*You can easily buy peach puree; it is sold in small portions since it's often given to babies. Otherwise, you can prepare it yourself by blending fresh or canned peaches.

(1) Fill a metal shaking tin with ice, mezcal, peach puree, pineapple juice, simple syrup 2:1, and prosecco.

(2) Throw the liquid between the large and the small tin of the shakers 4 or 5 times to give aeration to the cocktail.

(3) Pour it into a chilled flute, and then top up with prosecco.

(4) Squeeze a lemon coin over glass and then discard it.

Bartender's Tip: *Pair Peachy Bubbles with a sweet brunch. It is fantastic with pancakes and caramel sauce, which will enhance the aroma and the tasting notes of the Ilegal Reposado. Or try a chocolate cake layered with orange marmalade to prolong the Ilegal Reposado's finishing notes, which will leave a zesty, choco-tastic aftertaste.*

PLUMEE

Tasting notes: sparkling, fruity, and dry

This is a low-ABV cocktail made for those who want to start their brunch with something exquisite, with fruity notes. It becomes sparkling once you add CO_2, softening all the flavors and making it even more delicate.

YIELD: 4 COCKTAILS

2 ounces (60 ml) tequila

2 ounces (60 ml) dry vermouth

3⅓ ounces (100 ml) umeshu,* such as Choya

4 ounces (12 0ml) lychee juice

2 teaspoons (7.5 ml) Tartaric and Malic Solution 6% (page 215)

1 maraschino cherry

*Umeshu is a Japanese liqueur with a sweet-and-sour taste.

(1) Combine tequila, dry vermouth, umeshu, lychee juice, and tartaric and malic solution 6% in a jar.

(2) Pour the liquid into the soda siphon and fill it with CO_2.

(3) Store it in the fridge for 1 hour before serving it.

(4) Pour the chilled, sparkling liquid into a chilled single rocks glass.

(5) Garnish with a maraschino cherry.

Bartender's Choice: *Go for a light and refreshing tequila, such as Espolon Blanco, in the Plumee; a strong, flavored tequila will overwhelm the light fruity notes of lychee juice and umeshu.*

SPICY, TIGER!

Tasting notes: spicy, fruity, and refreshing

What is better than sharing a cocktail with your friends? This cocktail is inspired by a classic Mai Tai. It is delicious and has the right spiciness to light up your brunch. You can mix it with a regular ginger beer but, trust me, the result will be much better with a homemade one.

YIELD: 5 COCKTAILS

6¾ ounce (200 ml) mezcal, such as Quiquiriqui

2½ ounce (75 ml) Avocado Pit Orgeat* (page 218)

3⅓ ounce (100 ml) orange juice

1⅔ ounce (50 ml) Cointreau

10 ounces (300 ml) Homemade Ginger Beer (page 210), or store-bought

*Making Avocado Pit Orgeat takes time. So, if you are craving a Spicy, Tiger ASAP, you can buy a basic orgeat. It will slightly change the flavor of the cocktail, but it will still be delicious!

(1) Blend mezcal, avocado pit orgeat, orange juice, and Cointreau in a blender with one scoop of crushed ice.

(2) Pour it into an absinthe fountain or punch bowl filled with ice.

(3) Top up the fountain with ginger beer.

Bartender's Choice: *Because Spicy, Tiger! is based on sweet vegetal notes, I like to use Quiquiriqui mezcal, which is loaded with fruity elements. (Quiquiriqui is extremely versatile and you can enjoy it just by sipping it.)*

CHAPTER 2:
"AFTERNOON TEA"
COCKTAILS

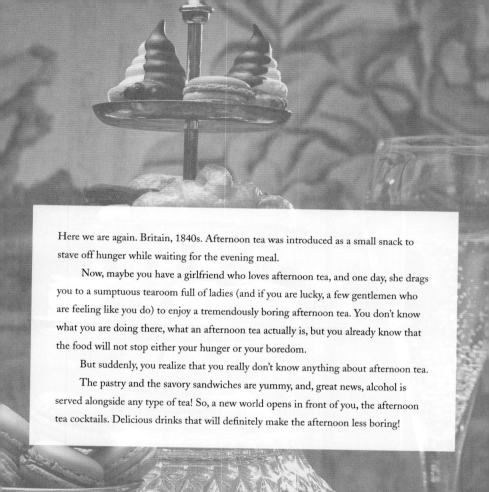

Here we are again. Britain, 1840s. Afternoon tea was introduced as a small snack to stave off hunger while waiting for the evening meal.

Now, maybe you have a girlfriend who loves afternoon tea, and one day, she drags you to a sumptuous tearoom full of ladies (and if you are lucky, a few gentlemen who are feeling like you do) to enjoy a tremendously boring afternoon tea. You don't know what you are doing there, what an afternoon tea actually is, but you already know that the food will not stop either your hunger or your boredom.

But suddenly, you realize that you really don't know anything about afternoon tea.

The pastry and the savory sandwiches are yummy, and, great news, alcohol is served alongside any type of tea! So, a new world opens in front of you, the afternoon tea cocktails. Delicious drinks that will definitely make the afternoon less boring!

AN ENGLISHMAN IN OAXACA

Tasting notes: citrus, fruity, and tannic

Inspired by my time spent in England, I decided to give a kick to a traditional tea to drink in the afternoon. The Earl Grey combined with tequila gives smoky bergamot flavor, cut with the agave's sweetness. From a picturesque tearoom, you will be transported to an agave field.

YIELD: 1 COCKTAIL

1½ ounces (45 ml) Earl Grey Tea-Infused Tequila (page 199)

¾ ounce (25 ml) apple cider vinegar

⅔ ounce (20 ml) freshly squeezed lemon juice

1 teaspoon (10 ml) agave nectar

2 lemon macarons

(1) Fill and chill a mixing glass or a metal shaking tin with ice.

(2) Pour Earl Grey tea-infused tequila, apple cider vinegar, lemon juice, and agave nectar into the chilled vessel and stir rapidly with a bar spoon for 17 to 20 seconds.

(3) Strain into a chilled teacup.

(4) Garnish with a couple of lemon macarons. Serve them on the side in a small saucers, matching your cup.

BLACK SUNSET

Tasting notes: peppery, citrusy, and smoky

Inspired by a long summery drink to have on the beach, this fizzy cocktail will take you to a whole new level. A triumph of aromas, well balanced and very intense. It is a long drink, so sip it slowly and take your time to taste each ingredient. Let them tell you a beautiful story of their Asian flavors.

YIELD: 1 COCKTAIL

1⅔ ounces (50 ml) Sichuan Peppercorn-Infused Mezcal (page 205)

⅔ ounce (20 ml) yuzu juice

2 dashes aromatic bitters

3⅓ ounces (100 ml) Lapsang Souchong Tea Soda (page 211)

1 yuzu coin

(1) Fill and chill a mixing glass or a metal shaking tin with ice.

(2) Pour Sichuan peppercorn-infused mezcal, yuzu juice, and aromatic bitters into the vessel and stir rapidly with a bar spoon for 17 to 20 seconds.

(3) Strain into a chilled highball over ice.

(4) Top up with chilled lapsang souchong tea soda.

(5) Garnish with a yuzu coin.

Bartender's Tip: *Go for yuzu juice instead of the classic lemon juice. Yuzu is more delicate and a perfect match for a cocktail made with Asian ingredients.*

CANDY FIZZ

Tasting notes: creamy, sweet, fizzy

Do not be fooled by the ingredients or the name because Candy Fizz is not as sweet as it may seem. On the contrary, it is well balanced between sweet and fruity, and you will not be able to resist it. Candy Fizz is a yummy cocktail to drink with your afternoon tea.

YIELD: 1 COCKTAIL

1½ ounces (45 ml) tequila

⅓ ounce (10 ml) Aperol

⅓ ounce (10 ml) Amaretto Disaronno

⅓ ounce (10 ml) Apple Syrup (page 216)

⅓ ounce (10 ml) Marshmallow Syrup (page 237)

¾ ounce (25 ml) egg white

Top up with soda

1 marshmallow to garnish

(1) Combine tequila, Aperol, Amaretto Disaronno, apple syrup, marshmallow syrup, and egg white. Dry shake (without ice) for 10 seconds.

(2) Add ice to the shaker, close, and hard shake for 10 seconds until the shaker is frozen.

(3) Double strain into a chilled highball.

(4) Top up with soda.

(5) Garnish with a marshmallow (if you want, you can roast it first).

Make a mocktail Candy Fizz for your kids

You can make a wonderful mocktail version of the Candy Fizz. Your kids will love it, and who knows, maybe you will love it too!

Substitute tequila, Aperol, and Amaretto Disaronno with ⅓ cup (80 ml) apple juice and 1 ounce (30 ml) pineapple juice. Then follow the steps above. Now you have a drink to share with your whole family.

LA MAR

Tasting notes: sour, fruity, and fresh

Inspired by a classic Southside, La Mar is a very easy cocktail to drink. It is refreshing, with a dash of saltiness, which reminds me of a sea breeze. Everything in this cocktail will take you back to a summer day on the beach. The caraway adds an herbal and a sharp taste, and it brightens the drink with an anise aroma. Each ingredient is chosen to cure hot weather. It turns sweet from the cordial and fresh from the cucumber. It gets acidity from the fresh lime juice and gains a minty note from, of course, mint leaves.

YIELD: 1 COCKTAIL

6 mint leaves

1⅓ ounces (40 ml) mezcal, such as Ilegal Joven

¾ ounce (25 ml) freshly squeezed lime juice

⅔ ounce (20 ml) apple juice

½ ounce (15 ml) Cucumber & Caraway Cordial (page 189)

1 cucumber slice

(1) Combine mint leaves, mezcal, lime juice, apple juice, and cucumber and caraway cordial in a small metal shaker tin.

(2) Fill with ice cubes until the top and close the shaker. Hard shake for 10 seconds until the shaker is frozen.

(3) Double strain into a chilled double rocks glass over a block of ice.

(4) Garnish with a cucumber slice.

Bartender's Choice: *Ilegal Joven is an excellent choice for this drink because it highlights the cocktail's freshness, bringing up mineral and herbal notes already from the aroma and making it an excellent cocktail for those who love light and crispy drinks, such Mojito and Mint Julep.*

MEZCAL FEVER

Tasting notes: fruity, sweet, and citrus

This drink is a summer tiki mug perfect for any occasion! Are you melting on the beach? Get a Mezcal Fever. Are you getting ready for dinner? Drink a Mezcal Fever while you put on your best suit! This cocktail will drive you crazy, just like a fever! An explosion of fruitiness that meets the strength of smoky mezcal and the delicacy of honey.

YIELD: 1 COCKTAIL

---

15 mint leaves

1⅓ ounces (40 ml) mezcal, such as Ilegal Reposado

½ ounce (15 ml) rhubarb liqueur

⅔ ounce (20 ml) pineapple juice

⅔ ounce (20 ml) freshly squeezed lime juice

2 teaspoons (10 ml) Honey Water 2:1 (page 235)

1 Maraschino cherry (store-bought, or see page 176 for Homemade Cherry Blend)

1 lime wedge

3 pineapple leaves

(1) Combine mint leaves, mezcal, rhubarb liqueur, pineapple juice, lime juice, and honey water in a small metal shaker tin.

(2) Fill with ice cubes until the top and close the shaker. Hard shake for 10 seconds until the shaker is frozen.

(3) Double strain into a tiki mug. Fill with crushed ice to the top.

(4) Garnish with a cherry, lime wedge, and three pineapple leaves.

Bartender's Choice: *For this cocktail, go for a mezcal full of character, such as Ilegal Reposado. Fruity aromas at the nose, a soft wood smoke on the palate, and an oaky finish will create the perfect picture.*

QUIET CHAOS

Tasting notes: smoky, citrus, and spiced

Here is your new favorite cup of tea in disguise! Have your tea combined with the strength of mezcal, the spiciness of ginger, and the bitterness of a fantastic fruity syrup. The Quiet Chaos is a refreshing cocktail, amazing paired with savory sandwiches. A real treat!

YIELD: 1 COCKTAIL

1½ ounces (45 ml) mezcal, such as Cobre Negro

½ ounce (15 ml) Chamomile Dry Vermouth (page 195)

⅓ ounce (10 ml) store-bought or homemade Ginger Juice (page 232)

½ ounce (15 ml) Grapefruit & Peychaud Syrup (page 228)

Sunflower Seed and Almond Praline (page 185)

(1) Fill a mixing glass or a metal shaking tin with ice.

(2) Pour mezcal, chamomile dry vermouth, ginger juice, and Grapefruit & Peychaud Syrup into the chilled vessel, stir rapidly with a bar spoon for 17 to 20 seconds.

(3) Strain into a chilled single rocks glass over a block of ice.

(4) Garnish with sunflower seed and almond praline.

A Mezcal to Know: The Cobre Negro project started in 2020 when the producer decided to make mezcal more accessible to any palate. That is why Cobre Negro is made with wild Tepeztate agave, which, through the artisanal method, gets a smooth and sweet flavor. Cobre Negro is great for a Quiet Chaos, so full of flavors, where spiced, bitter, sour, and sweet live in perfect harmony.

RED RHUBY

Tasting notes: fruity, sweet, and crisp

This is a low-ABV cocktail for those who want to enjoy a drink during an afternoon tea. Pair it with pastry or pies; it will be a yummy combination. Light, delicate, and full of flavors, it is one of those cocktails you can never say no to.

YIELD: 1 COCKTAIL

1 ounce (30 ml) tequila

⅔ ounce (20 ml) Aperol

½ ounce (15 ml) rhubarb liqueur, such as Giffard

⅓ ounce (10 ml) dry vermouth

1 ounce (30 ml) peach tea, brewed and chilled

1 Maraschino cherry (store-bought or see page 176 for Homemade Cherry Blend)

(1) Fill a mixing glass or a metal shaking tin with ice.

(2) Pour tequila, Aperol, rhubarb liqueur, dry vermouth, and peach tea into the chilled vessel, and stir rapidly with a bar spoon for 17 to 20 seconds.

(3) Strain into a chilled coupette glass.

(4) Garnish with a Maraschino cherry.

SINGLE LADIES

Tasting notes: fruity, dry, and sparkling

Do you want to make your regular champagne interesting for your afternoon party? Here's a Single Ladies! The mezcal will spice up your drink and still give you that bubbly effect we all love in champagne. Besides, the cocktail will open up your appetite, and it will be an excellent pairing with savory tea sandwiches.

YIELD: 1 COCKTAIL

1¼ ounces (35 ml) tequila, such as Espolon Blanco

1⅔ ounces (50 ml) pear juice

⅓ ounce (10 ml) Simple Syrup 2:1 (page 242)

Top up with champagne

Clear Pear (page 178)

(1) Fill a metal shaking tin with ice, tequila, pear juice, and simple syrup 2:1.

(2) Throw the liquid between the large and the small tin of the shakers 4 or 5 times to aerate the cocktail.

(3) Pour it into a flute and top up with champagne.

(4) Garnish with a clear pear.

Bartender's Choice: *Espolon Blanco has a light-medium body that allows the cocktails to be balanced and not overwhelmed by just the strong tequila flavor. It has pepper, vanilla, and grilled pineapple notes, culminating in a spiciness that hinders a little bit of the pear's sweetness.*

SUMMER FLUTE

Tasting notes: tropical, fresh, sparkling

There are not a lot of cocktails that combine mezcal and champagne. They might belong to two different worlds, but together they give an explosion of flavors. A balanced note of sweet, smoky, and fruity directly into a flute glass emphasizes the flavors.

YIELD: 1 COCKTAIL

1⅔ ounces (50 ml) Exotic Dried Fruits-Infused Mezcal (page 200), preferably made with Mezcal Lo Verás Joven

⅔ ounce (20 ml) pineapple juice

1½ teaspoon (7.5 ml) vanilla syrup (store-bought or see page 233 for Homemade Vanilla Syrup)

⅓ ounce (10 ml) freshly squeezed lime juice

Top up with champagne

(1) Combine exotic dried fruits–infused mezcal, pineapple juice, vanilla syrup, and lime juice into a small metal shaker tin.

(2) Fill with ice cubes to the top and close the shaker. Hard shake for 10 seconds until the shaker is frozen.

(3) Double strain into a chilled flute.

(4) Top up with champagne.

Bartender's Choice: *Mezcal Lo Verás Joven enhances the flavor of Summer Flute thanks to its tropical aroma and orange blossom and roast agave notes on the palate. A great choice that evokes tropical fruit aromas.*

SPECTRUM

Tasting notes: fruity, refreshing, long drink

The Spectrum is the perfect cocktail for those who love fruity drinks. It is very easy to make, and you will have so much fun while making it. Just push your fantasy and use any colorful fruits you have at home. Tonic water will combine the ingredients well. It is a sipping drink: the more the fruit ice cubes melt, the fruitier the cocktail will get.

YIELD: 1 COCKTAIL

1⅔ ounces (50 ml) mezcal, such as Alipus Santa Ana Del Rio

2 tablespoons green apple juice

2 tablespoons tangerine juice

2 tablespoons pineapple juice

2 tablespoons blueberry juice

2 tablespoons pink grapefruit

2 tablespoons blood orange

3⅓ ounces (100 ml) tonic water

Several pieces of rainbow-striped candy

(1) Pour each juice (green apple juice, tangerine juice, pineapple juice, blueberry juice, pink grapefruit juice, and blood orange juice) in its own spot of the ice cube tray and place it in the freezer overnight or until frozen.

(2) In a chilled highball glass, arrange the ice cubes according to the rainbow spectrum colors (if you can), and then pour mezcal over top.

(3) Top up with tonic water and garnish with rainbow stripes.

Bartender's Choice: *Alipus Santa Ana Del Rio is a great mezcal, ideal for this drink. It is fresh and with a complex structure that will stand among the different flavors of the fruits. The floral notes and its richness close a circle of perfect harmony.*

CHAPTER 3:
APERITIF
COCKTAILS

The ancestor of the modern aperitif appeared in the Middle Ages when medicinal drinks were served before the meal. Then, in 1796 in Turin, Italy, Antonio Carpano created the first sweet vermouth (called "sweet" even if it is mildly bitter). A few years later, the French Joseph Noilly made dry vermouth. And from there, it was all uphill. While Italy and France became rivals in vermouth production, aperitifs got their popularity in the social gatherings. Once they reached America, they took it off since bartenders started to mix them in cocktails.

From the Latin word *aperire* (to open), aperitifs include a wide range of drinks, from straight vermouth to cocktails, and they are meant to stimulate the appetite to get you ready for dinner.

Traditionally, aperitif cocktails tend to be light in alcohol and bitter on taste, which is why they are commonly served with salty appetizers.

Aperitif cocktails are drunk all around the world; you can have a Daiquiri or a Caipirinha or a Negroni. Just choose yours, while I picture myself drinking a mezcal-based aperitif on a summer day sitting under the blue Venetian sky.

A MARIO

Tasting notes: savory, strong, salty

*High in alcohol content and quite smoky, too, A Mario is not for everyone.
You can actually taste the pungent presence of the onion brine. To appreciate
it, the cocktail needs to be served icy cold. Sip it during an aperitif and pair
it with nuts.*

YIELD: 1 COCKTAIL

1⅓ ounces (40 ml) mezcal,
such as Madre Mezcal

½ ounce (15 ml) fino sherry

⅓ ounce (10 ml) onion brine,
from a jar of pickled onions

1 pickled onion

(1) Fill a mixing glass or a metal shaking
tin with ice.

(2) Pour mezcal, fino sherry, and onion
brine into the chilled vessel and stir
rapidly with a bar spoon for 17–20
seconds.

(3) Strain into a coupette.

(4) Garnish with a pickled onion.

*Bartender's Tip: Madre mezcal is herbal and peppery, but also it has got salty notes.
It is a good match for A Mario because a strong mezcal is needed for this equally
potent cocktail. So, do not go for a citrusy or sweet mezcal; they will just get lost in
the drink.*

BEES' GOLD

Tasting notes: sweet, sparkling, smoky

Bees' Gold is a refreshing cocktail. It is a good start for those who are approaching mezcal for the first time. The spirit's smokiness is softened a bit by the agave's sweetness, dandelion tea soda, and lemon, making the cocktail easy to drink. You can have it at any time, but don't miss it as an aperitif—perfect to start a sparkling night!

YIELD: 1 COCKTAIL

1⅔ ounces (50 ml) mezcal, such as Vago Ensamble En barro

3⅓ ounces (100 ml) dandelion tea, brewed and chilled

1 tablespoon (20 grams) agave nectar

Lemon wedge

(1) Combine dandelion tea and agave nectar in a jar to make a dandelion tea soda. Pour the liquid into the soda siphon and fill it with CO_2.

(2) Store it in the fridge for 1 hour before serving it.

(3) Fill a skinny highball glass with ice and pour in mezcal.

(4) Shake the siphon and top up with dandelion tea.

(5) Garnish with a lemon wedge.

Bartender's Choice: *Vago Ensamble En barro is made by Solomon Ray Rodriguez in Sola De Vega, Oaxaca. It is a unique mezcal because each batch is made with ripe agaves that Tio Rey thinks are a good match, so every time, the agave selected ratios are different; thus, the mezcal is different. But generally, Ensambe En Barro is rich and earthy. For this unique mezcal, I created a delicate cocktail recipe, the Bees' Gold. The flavors are well matched without overwhelming one another.*

BERRY FIELD

Tasting notes: fruity, sweet, creamy

Berry Field is a low-ABV cocktail. Sloe gin releases notes of blackthorn berries which, combined with strawberry syrup, makes the drink fruity and sweet. Start your aperitif with a Berry Field; its delicate notes will not overwhelm the flavors of your meal.

YIELD: 1 COCKTAIL

¾ ounce (25 ml) mezcal, such as Alipus San Baltazar

¾ ounce (25 ml) sloe gin

⅔ ounce (20 ml) Strawberry Syrup (page 243)

⅔ ounce (20 ml) freshly squeezed lemon juice

¾ ounce (25 ml) egg white

1 slice of strawberry

(1) Combine mezcal, sloe gin, strawberry syrup, lemon juice, and egg white in a small metal shaker tin. Dry shake (without ice) for 10 seconds.

(2) Add ice cubes to the shaker, close, and hard shake for 10 seconds until the shaker is frozen.

(3) Double strain into a chilled highball.

(4) Garnish with a slice of strawberry.

Bartender's Choice: *Alipus is a series of mezcal selected and bottled by Los Danzantes distillery in order to preserve the mezcalero's role. Each edition takes the name from the town where it is distilled. Alipus San Baltazar, made from Espadín agave, gives fruity aromas and an accentuated roasted agave flavor, well balanced with sweet hints.*

FORBIDDEN PARADISE

Tasting notes: floral, sour, sweet

Sharp and fruity, but with a slightly bitter note, Forbidden Paradise is floral and refreshing. It's the right kick to start your aperitif and ideal for any palate. It is good with savory food, but also with chocolate!

Grapefruit, created by the union of sweet orange and pomelo in Barbados, was named forbidden fruit by Rev. Griffith Hughes in 1750. Later on, in 1830, it was re-named Citrus paradisi. From this, we get the name of this cocktail, the Forbidden Paradise.

YIELD: 1 COCKTAIL

1⅓ ounces (40 ml) tequila

⅓ ounce (10 ml) Aperol

⅓ ounce (10 ml) Yellow Chartreuse

⅔ ounce (20 ml) Grapefruit Sherbet* (page 229)

⅔ ounce (20 ml) freshly squeezed lime juice

1 grapefruit peel

*This grapefruit sherbet is a citrusy syrup that will take your cocktails to the next level.

(1) Combine tequila, Aperol, Yellow Chartreuse, grapefruit sherbet, and lime juice in a small metal shaker tin.

(2) Fill with ice cubes until the top and close the shaker. Hard shake for 10 seconds until the shaker is frozen.

(3) Double strain into a chilled coupette.

(4) Garnish with a grapefruit peel.

PINK JULEP

Tasting notes: fresh, smoky, citrus

This is a julep style drink, but Pink Julep has a smoky, sour, and bitter taste. It is a nice sipping cocktail. If you would like to pair it with food, go with shrimps and scallops, or opt for a Greek cheese-based appetizer or a feta salad.

YIELD: 1 COCKTAIL

---

6 mint leaves

1⅓ ounces (40 ml) mezcal, such as Ilegal Joven

⅔ ounce (20 ml) freshly squeezed pink grapefruit juice

⅓ ounce (10 ml) Agave Water 2:1 (page 217)

Pink grapefruit slice

1 mint sprig

(1) In a julep tin cup, very gently muddle the mint to release the essential oils. (Do not put too much energy into it; otherwise, mint will break without releasing any oil.)

(2) Pour in mezcal, pink grapefruit juice, and agave water. Half fill the cup with crushed ice and churn the drink with a bar spoon.

(3) Top up with more crushed ice and churn again.

(4) Repeat the process, so the drink fills the cup and frost forms on the outside. Once you build the drink, wait and let the cup get frosty. This could take at least 20–25 seconds or up to 1 minute.

(5) Slap the mint spring with your hands to release the aromatic oils. Garnish the cocktail with a grapefruit slice and one mint sprig.

Bartender's Choice: *Ilegal Joven, rich in agave flavors, highlights the Pink Julep's citrus and fruity notes, and also give a long bitter finish.*

LAYERS OF LOVE

Tasting notes: sweet, fruity, rich

Layers of Love is a sweet alternative to a classic Negroni. If you favor lighter drinks—and Negroni can be pretty strong for beginners—then you must try Layers of Love, a fruity cocktail with a vegetal hint from the Aperol's rhubarb. It's a very easy cocktail to drink that will help to prepare you for dinner.

YIELD: 1 COCKTAIL

---

1 ounce (30 ml) tequila, such as Tequila Ocho Blanco

1 ounce (30 ml) Aperol

⅔ ounce (20 ml) fraise liqueur (strawberry liqueur)

1 strawberry slice

(1) Fill a mixing glass or a metal shaking tin with ice.

(2) Pour tequila, Aperol, and fraise liqueur into the chilled vessel, and stir rapidly with a barspoon for 17 to 20 seconds.

(3) Strain into a chilled single rocks glass over a block of ice.

(4) Garnish with a strawberry slice.

Bartender's Choice: *Tequila Ocho Blanco is a good match for Layers of Love. It adds more flavor through its notes of citrus, cinnamon, and dried fruit. A spearmint hint on the finish is a great addition to the sweet flavors of the drink.*

MINESWEEPER FLOWER

Tasting notes: floral, light, smoky

Do you remember the Minesweeper game? You look for flags without finding mines. That is where I got the inspiration for this cocktail; in the Italian version of the game, you look for flowers and not flags. In this Minesweeper Flower drink, you definitely will look for and find a floral taste, but mind the good old smoky mezcal. The grapefruit foam adds a little bitterness to the drink, stimulating your appetite. Pair it with shrimp sandwiches or giant green olives. It will be a great aperitif.

YIELD: 1 COCKTAIL

¾ ounce (25 ml) mezcal, such as Alipus Santa Ana Del Rio

¾ ounce (25 ml) Suze

¾ ounce (25 ml) Yellow Chartreuse

Top up with Grapefruit Foam (page 180)

(1) Fill a mixing glass or a metal shaking tin with ice.

(2) Pour mezcal, Suze, and Yellow Chartreuse into the chilled vessel, stir rapidly with a barspoon for 17 to 20 seconds.

(3) Strain into a chilled Nick-and-Nora glass.

(4) Top up with grapefruit foam.

Bartender's Tip: *For a quick Minesweeper Flower, you can skip the grapefruit foam and instead serve the drink on the rocks with a grapefruit slice garnish.*

Bartender's Choice: *Alipus Santa Ana Del Rio, Suze, and Yellow Chartreuse are a hymn to spring: a combination of floral notes that will explode in your mouth, accompanied by a smoky note and a clean and refreshingly long finish thanks to the presence of Alipus Santa Ana Del Rio.*

SPICY SPRITZO

Tasting notes: spicy, aromatic, sparkling

With a mix of spiciness from chili and ginger, combined with the aromatic rose water, this cocktail will inebriate you. The Aperol and prosecco might remind you of a classic Aperol Spritz, but Spicy Spritzo, as the name suggests, is a spicier, hotter version of the Italian Aperitif par excellence.

YIELD: 1 COCKTAIL

⅔ ounce (20 ml) tequila

⅔ ounce (20 ml) Aperol

⅔ ounce (20 ml) Ginger Syrup

½ teaspoon (2.5 ml) rose water

2 drops Chili Tincture (page 187)

2 drops Saline Solution 10% (page 214)

Top up with prosecco

1 orange wedge

(1) Fill a chilled wine glass with ice.

(2) Combine tequila, Aperol, ginger syrup, rose water, chili tincture, and saline solution 10% in the glass.

(3) Gently stir and top up with prosecco.

(4) Garnish with an orange wedge.

THE SMOKY ARTICHOKE

Tasting notes: bitter, herbal, citrus

The Smoky Artichoke is a level-up of the Negroni with herbal notes from Fernet Branca and a smoky touch from mezcal, perfectly combined with Orange Ice that releases its flavor during the dilution process. If you like bitter and strong cocktails, this may be the one for you.

For an even smokier, peated drink, you can smoke this drink with apple wood chips.

YIELD: 1 COCKTAIL

---

1 ounce (30 ml), mezcal, such as Ilegal Reposado

⅔ ounce (20 ml) Campari

1 ounce (30 ml) Cynar

⅓ ounce (10 ml) Fernet Branca

2 dashes Peychaud's Bitters

1 block Orange Ice (page 182)

(1) Fill a chilled mixing glass or a metal shaking tin with ice.

(2) Add mezcal, Campari, Cynar, Fernet Branca, and Peychaud's Bitters, and stir rapidly with a bar spoon for 17 to 20 seconds.

(3) Put a block of orange ice into a double rocks glass and strain the drink over it.

(4) Garnish with an orange wedge.

Bartender's Choice: I particularly like this drink with Ilegal Reposado mezcal because it provides a woody and baked agave aroma to the nose. At the palate, it gives pipe tobacco, agave, and dry herbal notes. The Ilegal distillery is respectful of the environment and careful to use raw materials, meaning no artificial flavors or colorings are used in the production process. No matter what mezcal you use, the Smoky Artichoke is a slow sipping drink. The more it dilutes, the more orange flavor you get from the ice.

VIOLETTE

Tasting notes: citrus, floral, long drink

The Violette is a twist on the classic Aviation; because it is made with mezcal, you get smoky notes alongside the delicate floral hints. The presence of an Italian red bitter liqueur adds a bittersweet flavor to the cocktail, making it perfect for an aperitif. It's a very refreshing drink that is a great painkiller for hot weather.

YIELD: 1 COCKTAIL

---

1 ounce (30 ml) mezcal, such as Cobre Negro

⅓ ounce (10 ml) Italian red bitter liqueur

⅓ ounce (10 ml) violette liqueur

⅔ ounce (20 ml) freshly squeezed lime juice

1 teaspoon (5 ml) Simple Syrup 2:1 (page 242)

Top up with tonic water

1 lime wedge

(1) Combine mezcal, Italian red bitter liqueur, violette liqueur, lime juice, and simple syrup 2:1 in a small metal shaker tin.

(2) Fill with ice cubes until the top and close the shaker. Hard shake for 10 seconds until the shaker is frozen.

(3) Fill a chilled highball with ice and double strain the cocktail into it.

(4) Top up with tonic water.

(5) Garnish with a lime wedge sitting on the ice.

Cobra Negro was created to be a less smoky mezcal. The distillery uses wild Tepeztate agave, which gives sweet notes to the final product. In the Violette cocktail, Cobre Negro adds a silky texture and enhances the drink's sweet, floral notes.

CHAPTER 4:
DINNER COCKTAILS

Historically, dinner was the largest meal of the day, whether it was daytime or evening. Nowadays, we associate it with the evening meal (most of us, at least). Fish, meat, and veggie dishes are commonly served with beer, or white or red wine. Some fizzy never spoils the party. But today, even cocktails are getting their spot on the table.

I know, pairing drinks and food is not easy. But a little bit of common sense and a general rule of thumb should save your time and dinner. If the cocktail and the food share one ingredient, then you are good to go. Plus, remember that spirits absorb fat and clean the palate, preparing you for the next course.

The next time you are eating a nicely marbled ribeye, do not clean and refresh your mouth with a salad; instead, think about a cocktail, or even better, a tequila-based cocktail.

A TROPICAL WINTER

Tasting notes: sweet, fruity, smoky

Here's a summer cocktail to have with your dinner. It is exquisite, and the flavors will transport you to a tropical island. Let you seduce by the sweetness of the fruits that goes so well alongside a wintery touch of anise.

YIELD: 1 COCKTAIL

1⅔ ounces (50 ml) Star Anise-Infused Mezcal (page 207), made with Vago Elote Aquilino

2 ½ tablespoons or 1⅓ ounces (40 ml) watermelon juice

⅔ ounce (20 ml) freshly squeezed lime juice

⅔ ounce (20 ml) Clear Banana Syrup (page 224)

1 star anise

(1) Combine star anise-infused mezcal, watermelon juice, lime juice, and clear banana syrup in a small metal shaker tin.

(2) Fill with ice cubes until the top and close the shaker. Hard shake for 10 seconds until the shaker is frozen.

(3) Place a block of ice into a chilled single rocks glass and double strain the cocktail into it.

(4) Garnish with star anise.

Bartender's Tip: *Banana syrup is an easy one to make. But, if you crave A Tropical Winter for your dinner, and you do not have time to make the banana syrup, then check your local shops. You can easily find it there.*

Vago Elote *is a great mezcal choice here. Produced by Aquilino Garcia Lopez, it is made of Espadín agave and infused with toasted corn. It amplifies the tropical flavors of this drink, thanks to its unripened banana and papaya hints. But it also gives something extra: a smoky and refreshing finish that cuts a bit of the sweetness of the cocktail.*

AN OCEAN BETWEEN US

Tasting notes: sweet, fruity, dry

This is the point where Mexico and Japan meet. A combination of cleanliness from tequila and the sweetness of umeshu. But do not get fooled by the ingredients because An Ocean Between Us can look like an easy cocktail to drink, which it is, but it is also a strong one. It will explode in your mouth, releasing all its flavors. Drink it while eating tacos; it will be delicious!

YIELD: 1 COCKTAIL

1⅔ ounces (50 ml) tequila

½ ounce (15 ml) umeshu, such as Choya

⅓ ounce (10 ml) Demerara Sugar Syrup (page 226)

2 dashes chocolate bitters

1 lemon peel

(1) Fill a mixing glass or a metal shaking tin with ice.

(2) Pour tequila, umeshu, demerara sugar syrup, and chocolate bitters into the chilled vessel, and stir rapidly with a bar spoon for 17 to 20 seconds.

(3) Strain into a chilled coupette.

(4) Garnish with a lemon peel.

CAB & MEG

Tasting notes: spiced, sweet, savory

The Cab & Meg is born when the fresh flavor of a cabbage meets nutmeg's pungent aroma, making a fantastic and light dinner cocktail. Cabbage and nutmeg are a natural pairing that give a sweet touch to the drink as well. Do not feel too bad if you do not eat your vegetables with your meal, because now you can have Cab & Meg instead!

YIELD: 1 COCKTAIL

1⅓ ounces (40 ml) mezcal, such as Alipus Santa Ana Del Rio

⅓ ounce (10 ml) dry vermouth

⅓ ounce (10 ml) crème de cacao blanc

⅔ ounce (20 ml) Cabbage & Nutmeg Shrub (page 220)

(1) Fill a mixing glass or a metal shaking tin with ice.

(2) Pour mezcal, dry vermouth, crème de cacao blanc, and cabbage & nutmeg shrub into the chilled vessel. Stir rapidly with a bar spoon for 17 to 20 seconds.

(3) Strain into a Nick-and-Nora glass.

Bartender's Choice: *Alipus Santa Ana Del Rio has a complex structure that will give smoky, mineral notes to the cocktail. Plus, its fresh, savory profile pairs beautifully with the cabbage & nutmeg shrub. But Cab & Meg will also please those who are looking for a light, sweet cocktail; crème de cacao blanc adds a touch of sweetness to this very delicate drink.*

CALL ME FLOWER

Tasting notes: sweet, citrus, savory

Not a drink for everyone. Call me flower is for a palate that wants to experiment with something new and different. Black pepper, hidden in the syrup, will enhance the cauliflower's flavor. It is best to drink when it is really cold to taste every single note of this sensational drink.

YIELD: 1 COCKTAIL

1⅔ ounces (50 ml) tequila, such as Tequila Ocho Reposado

⅔ ounce (20 ml) Cauliflower Jelly Syrup (page 221)

⅓ ounce (10 ml) freshly squeezed lime juice

2 dashes orange bitters

(1) Combine tequila, cauliflower jelly syrup, freshly squeezed lime juice, and orange bitters in a small metal shaker tin.

(2) Fill with ice cubes to the top and close the shaker. Hard shake for 10 seconds until the shaker is frozen.

(3) Double strain into a large chilled coupette.

A perfect pairing: Tequila Ocho Reposado is the right tequila for Call Me Flower. Smell the drink before you drink it: the floral and the sweet, cooked agave notes will inebriate you. Then take a sip: you will be welcomed by the cauliflower jelly syrup, then walk through with some citrus and oak notes and walk away with a slight note of a bittersweet hint which will last on the palate for quite a while.

HOT LIKE HELL

Tasting notes: spicy, fruity, refreshing

Here it comes, your summer pal! Hot Like Hell is the type of cocktail that you drink one after another. You will have it as an aperitif, maybe during a light dinner, and why not, during a brunch as well! It is one of those cocktails so delicious that you will find a way to pair it with any food you eat. Do not let the name or the chilies presence fool you: this cocktail is refreshing. It's also a little bit sweet and, of course, slightly spicy. A harmony of flavors to color your summer!

YIELD: 1 COCKTAIL

---

4 fresh raspberries

12 mint leaves

1⅔ ounces (50 ml) tequila or mezcal

½ ounce (15 ml) raspberry liqueur

¾ ounce (25 ml) freshly squeezed lime juice

⅓ ounce (10 ml) Chili Cordial (page 187)

2 mint springs

1 fresh chili

(1) Combine raspberries, mint leaves, tequila or mezcal, raspberry liqueur, lime juice, and chili cordial into a small metal shaker tin.

(2) Fill with ice cubes to the top and close the shaker. Hard shake for 10 seconds until the shaker is frozen.

(3) Double strain into a chilled highball and cover it with crushed ice to the top of the glass.

(4) Garnish with mint springs and a fresh chili.

Bartender's Choice: *Either with tequila or mezcal, Hot Like Hell will be delicious. If you prefer a smoother cocktail, go for tequila. But if you are looking for something stronger and smoking, go for mezcal. Do not muddle raspberries and mint; if you do a proper hard shake, they will break and release their flavor. A double strain will do the rest, avoiding the pulp and small pieces from falling into the glass.*

POSY

Tasting notes: citrus, herbal, floral

This cocktail showcases the elegance of mezcal and at the same time, gives an herbal and flower bouquet aroma, accompanied by a sweet apricot flavor. But it is not all about sweetness: the Green Chartreuse and citric acid presence give it a citrusy taste.

YIELD: 1 COCKTAIL

1⅓ ounces (40 ml) mezcal, such as Madre Mezcal

⅔ ounce (20 ml) Green Chartreuse*

⅓ ounce (10 ml) apricot brandy

1½ teaspoons (7.5 ml) citric acid solution 10% (page 212)

1 teaspoon (5 ml) Simple Syrup 2:1 (page 242)

1 grapefruit coin

Baby's breath flowers to garnish

*Green Chartreuse is a French liqueur made with 132 botanicals. You can imagine the blast of flavor in the mouth. You can use it to make so many classic cocktails and twist. With floral and vegetal notes, it is an excellent contribution to your brunches and aperitives.

(1) Fill a mixing glass or a metal shaking tin with ice and chill.

(2) Pour mezcal, Green Chartreuse, apricot brandy, citric acid solution 10%, and simple syrup 2:1 into the vessel and stir rapidly with a bar spoon for 17 to 20 seconds.

(3) Strain into a chilled coupette.

(4) Squeeze a grapefruit coin on the top of the glass and discard it.

(5) Garnish with a sprig of baby's breath.

Bartender's Tip: Think carefully about the choice of the mezcal you want to use in the Posy. I went for Madre Mezcal because not only does it have floral notes, which mirror and enhance the Green Chartreuse, but also because it has lovely smoke and pepper notes that create a balance and a good contrast.

SAMPHIRE COLLINS

Tasting notes: refreshing, citrus, sparkling

A refreshing cocktail with sweet notes and a strong flavor of tequila, a Samphire Collins is great for spring and summertime. It's a twist on a classic Tom Collins, with an extra salty kick that will quench your thirst and make you wish that summer could last forever.

YIELD: 1 COCKTAIL

1⅔ ounces (50 ml) tequila

⅔ ounce (20 ml) freshly squeezed lime juice

1 ounce (30 ml) Samphire Oleo Saccharum (page 241)

2 dashes Saline Solution 10% (page 214)

3⅓ ounces (100 ml) soda water

2 samphire*

*Samphire has vibrant green stalks and a crisp, salty taste. It's delicious in cocktails, but also in many recipes.

(1) Combine tequila, lime juice, samphire oleo saccharum, and saline solution 10% in a small metal shaker tin.

(2) Fill with ice cubes until the top and close the shaker. Hard shake for 10 seconds until the shaker is frozen.

(3) Fill a chilled highball with ice and double strain the cocktail into it.

(4) Top up with soda water, and garnish with samphire.

WILD PIG

Tasting notes: smoky, citrus, sweet

The Wild Pig is a fantastic addition to any dinner. It will light up your meal. Do not be fooled by the presence of the bacon; with its acidity and smokiness, the Wild Pig will clean your palate and get you ready for another course! But do not forget to leave some room for dessert!

YIELD: 1 COCKTAIL

1 ounce (30 ml) Bacon Fat–Washed Mezcal (page 191)

½ ounce (15 ml) dry vermouth

½ ounce (15 ml) Citrus Peel Syrup (page 223)

¾ ounce (25 ml) freshly squeezed lemon juice

1 chocolate pig stamp,* optional

*For how to crown your cocktails with lovely chocolate stamps, see page 179. It's easier than you think.

(1) Combine bacon fat–washed mezcal, dry vermouth, citrus peel syrup, and lemon juice into a small metal shaker tin.

(2) Fill with ice cubes until the top and close the shaker.

(3) Hard shake for 10 seconds until the shaker is frozen.

(4) Double strain into a chilled Nick-and-Nora.

(5) Garnish with a chocolate pig stamp if desired.

CHAPTER 5:
DIGESTIF COCKTAILS

Appearing on the dining table in the eighteenth century, the digestif was introduced to calm the stomach; that is why they were basically elixirs mixed with herbs and spices. If aperitifs help to stimulate your appetite, digestifs help to wind down and digest your meal. They are typically sweet but can also be herbal and bitter to please every palate. From amaros to fortified wines, today even cocktails can be considered a digestif.

Digestifs have a higher alcohol content and an elevated presence of sugar, which is why they can also be drunk as a replacement for dessert. Think about it: you just finished a heavy Italian dinner, you don't want to see food for at least forty-eight hours, but here comes the dessert. A beautiful and delicious cake will give you closure but will make you explode. Or you can go for the digestif cocktail, which won't make you feel too bad; on the contrary, it will give you a nice, relaxed feeling.

So, which is my favorite dessert? Tiramisù? No, too predictable. Ice cream? Well, I wouldn't say no, but I will always prefer a good digestif cocktail instead of dessert.

JIMADOR SOUL

Tasting notes: buttery, coffee, nutty

A smooth and nutty drink with a coffee finish, the Jimador Soul will guide you all night long through a sweet pleasure that you have never tried before. It will become your favorite digestif!

YIELD: 1 COCKTAIL

---

1 ounce (30 ml) Homemade Pistachio Butter-Washed Mezcal (page 204), made with Ilegal Reposado

¾ ounce (25 ml) coffee liqueur, such as Kahlua

¾ ounce (25 ml) chocolate liqueur

2 dashes aromatic bitters

¾ ounce (25 ml) still water, optional, if preparing in a bottle in advance

1 white chocolate feather stamp*, optional

*It's actually quite easy to make chocolate stamp garnishes for your cocktails. See page 179.

(1) Fill a mixing glass or a metal shaking tin with ice.

(2) Pour mezcal, coffee liqueur, chocolate liqueur, and aromatic bitter in the chilled vessel, stir rapidly with a bar spoon for 17 to 20 seconds.

(3) Strain over a block of ice in a chilled double rocks glass or pour into a small bottle to prepare in advance; if preparing in advance, also add 25 ml of still water to the small bottle, so that when poured int a glass, it is already diluted and can be served without ice.

(4) Garnish with a white chocolate feather stamp if desired.

Bartender's Choice: This cocktail is excellent with Ilegal Reposado because of its sweet notes of caramel, and soft wood smoke, combined with a chocolate liqueur. It gives a sensational pleasure to your mouth.

A MIDDAY AFFAIR

Tasting notes: creamy, tropical, sweet

This drink is a twist on the classic Piña Colada, with a more intense flavor of tequila. Instead of coconut milk, go for coconut sorbet because it gives more freshness and a strongest coconut note. Pineapple and coconut together will remind you of tropical dreams.

YIELD: 1 COCKTAIL

1⅔ ounces (50 ml) tequila

4 tablespoon (60 ml) Coconut Sorbet (page 225) or store-bought

⅚ ounce (25 ml) pineapple juice

⅔ ounce (20 ml) freshly squeezed lime juice

½ ounce (15 ml) Simple Syrup 2:1 (page 242)

3 pineapple leaves

1 maraschino cherry

1 lime wedge

(1) Combine tequila, homemade coconut sorbet, pineapple juice, lime juice, and simple syrup 2:1 in a small metal shaker tin.

(2) Fill with ice cubes until the top and close the shaker. Hard shake for 10 seconds until the shaker is frozen.

(3) Fill a chilled sling glass with ice and double strain the cocktail into it.

(4) Garnish with 3 pineapple leaves, maraschino cherry, and a lime wedge.

Go for a Virgin Colada too!

Here's a fantastic mocktail for when you do not want to have a drink or you just want to enjoy it with your kids.

*Go for the same recipe, but instead of the alcohol content, make the **Colada Kid** mocktail with 1⅔ ounces (50 ml) pineapple and ⅔ ounce (20 ml) Simple Syrup 2:1. Try it and adjust it to your taste.*

BERGAMIA

Tasting notes: fruity, delicate, sweet

Bergamia is an explosion of citrus flavors in your mouth. It is delicate and suitable for those who don't like strong cocktails. The final touch of bergamot oil is reminiscent of a classic earl grey tea, which is why you can have Bergamia at an afternoon tea. But that's not all. Being sweet, this cocktail is ideal for drinking while you have a dessert, too.

YIELD: 1 COCKTAIL

¾ ounce (25 ml) tequila, such as Tequila Ocho Reposado

⅔ ounce (20 ml) dry white wine

⅙ ounce (5 ml) umeshu, such as Choya

⅓ ounce (10 ml) freshly squeezed lime juice

1 teaspoon (5 ml) Simple Syrup 2:1 (page 242)

4 drops bergamot oil*

*If you cannot find bergamot oil, you can squeeze a lemon coin on the top of the glass to get a similar citrus aroma and flavor.

(1) Fill a mixing glass or a metal shaking tin with ice.

(2) Pour tequila, dry white wine, umeshu, lime juice, and simple syrup 2:1 into the chilled vessel and stir rapidly with a bar spoon for 17 to 20 seconds.

(3) Strain into a large chilled coupette.

(4) Garnish with drops of bergamot oil.

Bartender's Choice: *Tequila Ocho Reposado is an excellent addition to Bergamia, with its balanced notes of fruit and acidity. Plus, a soft tannin and an agave sweetness will linger on the finish, making the cocktail delicious. I recommend using a Pinot Grigio because it is a light dry white wine with fruity notes and slight citrus hints, making it a good match for Bergamia.*

AFTER GREEN

Tasting notes: creamy, sweet, minty

A twist on the classic Grasshopper, this cocktail is a great digestif cocktail. The mint's freshness is combined with the smokiness of mezcal, making the After Green strong and with an extra kick. It tastes like chocolate mint in cocktail form.

Make a big batch for a party. Just combine mezcal and crème de menthe. Once your guests arrive and you are ready for a cocktail or a dessert, add light cream. This is a very easy cocktail to make, and you can serve it as the final course of your dinner. The sweetness and freshness of the drink will please everyone.

YIELD: 1 COCKTAIL

1 ounce (30 ml) mezcal, such as Mezcal Lo Verás Reposado

1 ounce (30 ml) crème de menthe

2 tablespoons (30 ml) light cream*

1 chocolate mint thin, such as an After Eight

*If you want the cocktail to be even thicker, use heavy cream, or you can play a little bit with half-light and half-heavy cream. I recommend light cream because it is smoother.

(1) Combine mezcal, crème de menthe, and light cream in a small metal shaker tin.

(2) Fill with ice cubes to the top and close the shaker. Hard shake for 20 to 30 seconds until the shaker is frozen.

(3) Double strain into a chilled Irish coffee glass.

(4) Garnish with a chocolate mint thin.

Bartender's Choice: *Mezcal Lo Verás Reposado is made with 100% Agave Espadín. Produced in Oaxaca, notes of toffee and vanilla will embrace the sweetness of crème de menthe, making After Green a delightful cocktail.*

CORN FLIP

Tasting notes: sweet, creamy, spiced

Think about your movie night. You have candy, popcorn, a soda. But you feel like the movie you are watching requires a stronger and more intense drink. So, here's the Corn Flip. You get everything with it: sweet and spiced, smoky and salty. It will be unforgettable.

YIELD: 1 COCKTAIL

1⅓ ounces (40 ml) mezcal, such as Cobre Negro

⅓ ounce (10 ml) Amaro Montenegro

⅔ ounce (20 ml) crème de cacao dark

⅔ ounce (20 ml) store-bought or homemade Popcorn Syrup (page 239)

1 whole egg

2 drop Saline Solution 10% (page 214)

Popcorn to garnish

(1) Combine mezcal, Amaro Montenegro, crème de cacao dark, popcorn syrup, whole egg, and saline solution in a small metal shaker tin. Dry shake (without ice) for 10 seconds.

(2) Add ice to the shaker, close, and hard shake for 10 seconds until the shaker is frozen.

(3) Double strain into a chilled coupette, and garnish with a handful of popcorn.

Bartender's Tip: *Corn Flip is the ideal cocktail for those who have a sweet tooth. Cobre Negro Mezcal give an extra sweetness kick to the drink, making it suitable for those who just approached mezcal.*

CLAIRE TEMPTATION NO. 1

Tasting notes: sweet, fruity, smoky

Refreshing and delightful, Claire Temptation No. 1 is a great cocktail to finish off your dinner. It is rich, full of flavors, and a mix of tropical fruits combined with a gentle sweetness. Coconut, banana, and mezcal—nothing can go wrong. Claire Temptation No. 1 will take you to a tropical paradise.

YIELD: 1 COCKTAIL

1⅔ ounces (50 ml) Banana Chip-Infused Mezcal (page 192)

⅔ ounce (20 ml) crème de cacao white

⅔ ounce (20 ml) coconut water

1 teaspoon (5 ml) Citric Acid Solution 10% (page 212)

5 drops Malic Solution 10% (page 213)

½ ounce (15 ml) Clear Banana Syrup (page 224)

Banana chips

(1) Fill a mixing glass or a metal shaking tin with ice.

(2) Pour banana chip-infused mezcal, crème de cacao white, coconut water, citric acid solution 10%, malic solution 10%, and clear banana syrup into the chilled vessel; stir rapidly with a bar spoon for 17 to 20 seconds.

(3) Strain into a chilled double rocks glass over a cube of ice and garnish with banana chips.

Bartender's Tip: *If you do not have citric acid 10% and malic solution 10%, you can use 1 teaspoon (5 ml) of freshly squeezed lime juice instead. The color of the drink will be slightly different, more yellowish. Keep in mind that citric acid and malic solution make the cocktail clear and extend the cocktail's shelf life, making it last for longer in the place of freshly squeezed citrus.*

LADY MANHATTAN

Tasting notes: roasted agave, vegetal, sweet

Inspired by the classic Manhattan, this more delicate variation evokes dry oak and the Herradura Reposado's spiciness, one sip after another. You don't want to miss this drink's mixed sweet vegetal flavors if you are a sweet Manhattan lover.

YIELD: 1 COCKTAIL

1⅔ ounces (50 ml) Cherry-Infused Tequila (page 196), made with Herradura Reposado

⅔ ounce (20 ml) Cynar

⅓ (10 ml) maraschino liqueur

1 orange coin

1 maraschino cherry

(1) Fill and chill a mixing glass or a metal shaking tin with ice.

(2) Pour cherry-infused tequila, Cynar, and maraschino liqueur into the vessel and stir rapidly with a bar spoon for 17 to 20 seconds.

(3) Strain into a coupette and squeeze an orange coin on the top of the glass and discard it.

(4) Garnish with a maraschino cherry.

MOUNTAIN PATH

Tasting notes: herbal, sweet, spiced

Mountain Path will take you to the mountains. While drinking it, imagine yourself taking a long breath, immersed in the fresh air, and surrounded by green trees and wood smell. Herbal, liquorice, citrus—all in one drink. It feels like drinking in the mountain air.

YIELD: 1 COCKTAIL

1¼ ounces (35 ml) tequila

¼ ounce (7.5 ml) Fernet Branca

⅔ ounce (20 ml) Peppermint Dry Vermouth (page 202)

¼ ounce (7.5 ml) White Ale Reduction (page 209)

2 drops liquorice bitters

1 lemon coin, to squeeze and discard

(1) Fill a mixing glass or a metal shaking tin with ice.

(2) Pour tequila, Fernet Branca, peppermint dry vermouth, white ale reduction, and liquorice bitters into the chilled vessel, stir rapidly with a bar spoon between 17 to 20 seconds.

(3) Strain into a chilled Nick-and-Nora glass.

(4) Squeeze a lemon coin over the glass and discard it.

THE BOSS' WIFE

Tasting notes: spiced, fruity, citrus

Orange and apricot flavor pairs well with the smoky notes of mezcal, leaving a nice and long finish citrus note in your mouth. This drink is for sweet palates and for those who are looking for a small treat to finish off dinner. It's a refreshing, light, and easygoing drink to make.

YIELD: 1 COCKTAIL

⅔ ounce (20 ml) mezcal, such as Vago Elote Aquilino

⅔ ounce (20 ml) Amaro Del Capo

⅔ ounce (20 ml) apricot liqueur

⅔ ounce (20 ml) freshly squeezed lime juice

1 teaspoon (5 ml) Simple Syrup 2:1 (page 242)

1 orange coin to squeeze and discard

3 dried apricots

(1) Combine mezcal, Amaro Del Capo, apricot liqueur, lime juice, and simple syrup 2:1 in a small metal shaker tin.

(2) Fill with ice cubes to the top and close the shaker. Hard shake for 10 seconds until the shaker is frozen.

(3) Double strain into a chilled Nick-and-Nora glass. Squeeze an orange coin over the glass and discard it.

(4) Garnish with three dried apricots.

Bartender's Tip: *Vago Elote Aquilino is a good choice for the Boss' Wife. Starting from the aroma, it will contribute rich vanilla and earthy notes. Flavor-wise, it adds a nice touch of tropical fruit notes and sweet and nutty hints. Vago Elote Aquilino's particularity is that it is made with 100% agave Espadín and flavored with Mexican corn. Once toasted on a comal (a flat pan used for making tortillas), the corn is placed in the still with mezcal.*

PISTACHIO SOUR

Tasting notes: creamy, sour, coffee

Not a fan of espresso, but looking for something that can conclude your dinner? Here is the Pistachio Sour. Pistachio and coffee are a winning pair! With the addition of egg white, you will have a nice thick foam on the top, which will make the cocktail smooth and easy to drink—it will almost remind you of the Espresso Martini's foam.

YIELD: 1 COCKTAIL

1⅓ ounces (40 ml) Homemade Pistachio Butter-Washed Tequila (see page 204)

⅔ ounce (20 ml) coffee liqueur

⅔ ounce (20 ml) freshly squeezed lime juice

¾ ounce (25 ml) egg white

3 coffee beans

(1) Combine pistachio butter–washed tequila, coffee liqueur, lime juice, and egg white in a small metal shaker tin. Dry shake (without ice) for 10 seconds.

(2) Add ice cubes to the shaker, close, and hard shake for 10 seconds until the shaker is frozen.

(3) Double strain into a chilled coupette and garnish with 3 coffee beans.

Bartender's Tip: The homemade pistachio butter–washed tequila brings a delicate and nutty flavor to the drink and will brighten up the coffee notes. This will be an excellent union for the palate. It is unusual to have coffee and citrus elements in a drink, but Pistachio Sour will convince you how coffee can be versatile, working very well with many different ingredients. If you want it a little bit sweeter, you can add a little more coffee liqueur. But in this case, the ABV will rise too.

SWEET DREAMS

Tasting notes: sweet, herbal, nutty

This is a perfect cocktail to end a long day. It suits both those who love sweet and those who love a smoky drink. Chocolate and nutty flavors embrace well the herbal notes of Dom Benedictine. Give it a try as a replacement for dessert. You won't be disappointed.

If you have a sweet tooth, I suggest you dip few amaretti biscuits in dark chocolate to go with the cocktail.

YIELD: 1 COCKTAIL

1⅓ ounces (40 ml) Butter-Washed Mezcal, made with Los Amantes Reposado (page 194)

¼ ounce (7.5 ml) Dom Benedictine

⅓ ounce (10 ml) chocolate liqueur, such as Mozart

⅓ ounce (10 ml) Amaretto Disaronno

1 chocolate-dipped amaretti biscuit (page 177), if desired

(1) Fill and chill a mixing glass or a metal shaking tin with ice.

(2) Pour butter-washed mezcal, Dom Benedictine, chocolate liqueur, and Amaretto Disaronno into the vessel and stir rapidly with a bar spoon for 17 to 20 seconds.

(3) Strain into a chilled Nick-and-Nora glass.

(4) Garnish with a chocolate-dipped amaretti biscuit, if desired.

Bartender's Tip: Los Amantes Reposado has notes of sweet agave, vanilla, and light smoke, which pair well with a chocolate liqueur, such as Mozart chocolate liqueur. If you go for Los Amantes Reposado, do not mistaken it with Los Amantes Joven when you buy it. The flavors of these two mezcals are quite different: Los Amantes Reposado has sweet notes, whereas Los Amantes Joven has a citrus aroma that would completely change the flavor of a cocktail.

CHAPTER 6:
NIGHTCAP COCKTAILS

You are hanging out with your friends, you are having fun, and you want one last drink before saying goodnight and going to bed. But which drink? A shot of tequila? No, too quick. A mojito? Not the wisest choice on a winter night, maybe not on a summer night either if you have to go to bed after drinking it. You can't have an Aperol Spritz either, of course not (I guess?)! Then what?

Let me introduce you to the nightcap cocktails. Traditionally, a nightcap needs to warm you up before bed. A typical nightcap is a brown liquor, such as cognac and whiskey, something to sip slowly and relax you. Usually, they are served neat or warm, like a Hot Toddy or mulled wine.

But who says that a nightcap can't be a mezcal cocktail too? If you have arrived at this point in my book, you should know that I like experimenting and mixing. So, what's better than a nice mezcal nightcap?

AGA & PEPPE

Tasting notes: sweet, spiced, citrus

Aga & Peppe is the meeting of the sweetness of agave and the spiciness of peppercorn. It's a delicate but also pungent cocktail that has some serious punch. Pink peppercorn is a great match for tequila—it has a more delicate and sweeter flavor than other peppercorns.

YIELD: 1 COCKTAIL

1⅔ ounces (50 ml) tequila

⅓ ounce (10 ml) Pink Peppercorn & Agave Syrup (page 238)

2 dashes chocolate bitters

1 lemon peel

1 orange peel

(1) Fill a mixing glass or a metal shaking tin with ice.

(2) Pour tequila, pink peppercorn and agave syrup, and chocolate bitters into the chilled vessel; stir rapidly with a bar spoon for 17 to 20 seconds.

(3) Strain into a chilled double rocks glass over a cube of ice, and garnish with lemon and orange peel.

BACK TO SMOKE

Tasting notes: peppery, smoky, peated

If you like fruity or sweet cocktails, or if you just started to drink mezcal, this is not the drink for you. Back to Smoke is for those who love a smoky cocktail because everything in it is strong, intense, and peated. The best way to sip this drink is while you eat a small piece of dark chocolate and smoke a cigar—or at least that is how I drink it!

YIELD: 1 COCKTAIL

---

2 ounces (60 ml) Three Peppercorn-Infused Mezcal (page 208)

¼ ounce (7.5 ml) Lapsang Souchong Syrup 2:1 (page 236)

2 dashes angostura bitters

1 orange twist

(1) Fill a mixing glass or a metal shaking tin with ice.

(2) Pour three peppercorn-infused mezcal, lapsang souchong syrup 2:1, and angostura bitters into the chilled vessel; stir rapidly with a bar spoon for 17 to 20 seconds.

(3) Strain into a chilled double rocks glass over a cube of ice.

(4) Garnish with an orange twist.

BREATH CATCHER

Tasting notes: nutty, sweet, light

A delightful combo of ingredients makes this cocktail a pleasure for your senses. You will be captured by the aroma and then seduced by the flavors. It's a great nightcap cocktail that will make you melt with its sweetness.

YIELD: 1 COCKTAIL

1⅙ ounces (35 ml) tequila

½ ounce (15 ml) Amaretto Disaronno

⅓ ounce (10 ml) fino sherry

3 dashes Peychaud's Bitters

1 lemon peel

(1) Fill a mixing glass or a metal shaking tin with ice.

(2) Pour tequila, Amaretto Disaronno, fino sherry, and Peychaud's Bitters into the chilled vessel; stir rapidly with a bar spoon for 17 to 20 seconds.

(3) Strain into a chilled single rocks glass over a cube of ice.

(4) Garnish with lemon peel.

CLEME MY MIND

Tasting notes: bitter, strong, citrus

This cocktail is a twist on the classic Sazerac with a clementine note that adds flavor to the drink. Peychaud's bitters, aromatic bitters, and a clementine peel–infusion create a cozy, warm, winter feeling, making you want to drink a Cleme My Mind every night.

YIELD: 1 COCKTAIL

2 ounces (60 ml) Clementine Peel-Infused Mezcal (page 197)

2 dashes aromatic bitters

2 dashes Peychaud's Bitters

1 teaspoon (5 ml) Simple Syrup 2:1 (page 242)

5 drops absinthe, to rinse the glass

1 lemon peel

(1) Pour absinthe into a single rocks glass and fill it with crushed ice.

(2) Fill a mixing glass or a metal shaking tin with ice. Pour clementine peel–infuse mezcal, aromatic bitters, Peychaud's Bitters, and simple syrup 2:1 into the chilled vessel; stir rapidly with a bar spoon for 17 to 20 seconds.

(3) Throw the ice and absinthe away and strain the cocktail into the glass.

(4) Garnish with a lemon peel.

Bartender's Tip: When you rinse a glass with absinthe, you add an aniseed flavor to the cocktail, making it even stronger. It is a very nice touch to the drinks, such as a classic Sazerac and a Tuxedo No. 2.

MEZCAL FLIP

Tasting notes: spiced, creamy, smoky

Let me introduce you to your new winter cocktail. It's a sweet and enchanting drink that will drive you nuts. This flip-style cocktail is meant to be sipped in front of a crackling fireplace. It might be a little bit heavier than most nightcaps, but trust me, the sweet, dark, spiced flavors combined with the creaminess and a touch of smokiness will induce sleep!

YIELD: 1 COCKTAIL

1⅔ ounces (50 ml) mezcal, such as Cobre Negro

⅓ ounce (10 ml) crème de cacao blanc

1 ounce (30 ml) whole milk

⅔ ounce (20 ml) Cinnamon & Clove syrup (page 222)

1 whole egg

1 cinnamon stick

1 orange peel

(1) Combine mezcal, crème de cacao blanc, whole milk, cinnamon and clove syrup, and whole egg in a small metal shaker tin. Dry shake (without ice) for 10 seconds.

(2) Add ice cubes to the shaker, close, and hard shake for 10 seconds until the shaker is frozen.

(3) Double strain into a chilled double rocks glass over a block of ice.

(4) Garnish with cinnamon stick wrapped in orange peel.

Bartender's Tip: A gentle and smooth mezcal will be good for the Mezcal Flip. Cobre Negro adds green apple and dry fruits notes that will complement the syrup, enhancing each other. It's a light cocktail perfect for a delicate mezcal.

PARA TODO!

Tasting notes: herbal, citrus, smoky

Inspired by my mentor, this cocktail is a triumph of flavors. It is all a bartender could ask for! It is simply delicious, and it is the perfect drink after a very long day. It is very easy to make, so make two because the first will go very quickly. Best served very chilled.

YIELD: 1 COCKTAIL

¾ ounce (25 ml) mezcal, such as Vida Del Maguey

⅔ ounce (20 ml) Fernet Branca

⅔ ounce (20 ml) Agave Water 2:1 (page 217)

⅔ ounce (20 ml) freshly squeezed lemon juice

(1) Combine mezcal, Fernet Branca, agave water 2:1, and lemon juice in a small metal shaker tin.

(2) Fill with ice cubes to the top and close the shaker. Hard shake for 10 seconds until the shaker is frozen.

(3) Strain into a Nick-and-Nora glass.

Bartender's Tip: *Instead of Fernet Branca, you can also use Branca Menta if you like stronger herbal and mint notes.*

WISHING LEAF

Tasting notes: herbal, smoky, spiced

Maybe not the usual nightcap drink, but believe it or not, this cocktail will warm you up. Let yourself be embraced by the spiced and herbaceous notes of a magical combination of spirits. Take your time to sip and taste every single flavor. It is probably best to serve on a winter night but do not hesitate to drink it during summer.

YIELD: 1 COCKTAIL

1½ ounces (45 ml) Bay Leaf-Infused Mezcal (page 193), preferably made with Los Amantes Reposado

½ ounce (15 ml) Amaro Del Capo

¼ ounce (7.5 ml) Fernet Branca

2 dash orange bitters

1 bay leaf

(1) Fill and chill a mixing glass or a metal shaking tin with ice.

(2) Pour bay leaf–infused mezcal, Amaro Del Capo, Fernet Branca, and orange bitters into the vessel and stir rapidly with a bar spoon for 17 to 20 seconds.

(3) Strain into a chilled coupette.

(4) Garnish with a bay leaf on top of the glass.

Bartender's Choice: *When you choose a mezcal for the Wishing Leaf, avoid mezcals with citrus notes because they will not work well in this cocktail. Go, instead, for a warmer, winter flavored mezcal. Los Amantes Reposado is a good choice for its spiced and lightly sweet notes.*

YELLOW

Tasting notes: sweet, fruity, floral

If you are a sweet tooth, you will love Yellow. From the tropical notes to a kick of sweetness from the vanilla, it is a triumph of flavors. This is an excellent approach to mezcal if you are a beginner. This cocktail will accompany you on a relaxing night.

YIELD: 1 COCKTAIL

1⅔ ounces (50 ml) mezcal

⅓ ounce (10 ml) elderflower syrup

⅓ ounce (10 ml) mango puree

⅓ ounce (10 ml) freshly squeezed lime juice

¾ ounce (25 ml) egg white

⅓ ounce (10 ml) Homemade Vanilla Syrup (page 233), or store-bought

1 edible flower, such as a pansy or nasturtium

(1) Combine mezcal, elderflower syrup, mango puree, lime juice, egg white, and vanilla syrup in a small metal shaker tin. Dry shake (without ice) for 10 seconds.

(2) Add ice cubes to the shaker, close, and hard shake for 10 seconds until the shaker is frozen.

(3) Double strain into a coupette.

(4) Garnish with an edible flower.

Bartender's Tip: *Go for a mezcal without a complex structure; the Joven category is recommended because it will adapt more than other mezcals to Yellow's sweet and floral notes.*

APHRODISIAC OLD-FASHIONED

Tasting notes: rich, sweet, smoky

Here's a twist of a classic old-fashioned, but with the smoky flavor of mezcal. Chocolate and agave notes, accompanied by saffron hints, create a new drink, full of spiced aroma and a beautiful gold color. Let yourself be overwhelmed by the warmth of a cocktail that wants to celebrate love and passion through the use of chocolate and saffron, both aphrodisiac elements.

YIELD: 1 COCKTAIL

1⅔ ounces (50 ml) Butter-Washed Mezcal (page 194)

1 teaspoon (10 ml) agave nectar

¼ teaspoon (1 ml) Saffron Tincture (page 247)

2 dashes chocolate bitters

1 dash angostura bitters

1 dark chocolate stamp,* cactus-shaped or any other shape you like, optional

*For more on how to do a chocolate stamp garnish, flip to page 179.

(1) Fill a mixing glass or a metal shaking tin with ice.

(2) Pour butter-washed mezcal, agave nectar, saffron tincture, chocolate bitters, and angostura bitters into the chilled vessel, and stir rapidly with a barspoon for 17 to 20 seconds.

(3) Strain into a chilled single rocks glass over a block of ice.

(4) Garnish with a dark chocolate stamp, if desired. Just gently place it on top of the ice block (if you use ice cubes, leave it on the side, maybe placing it on a saucer).

THE INFAMOUS POME

Tasting notes: fruity, sweet, and sparkling

The Infamous Pome may look simple, but it is a complex drink: it has sweetness and fruitiness, but also a stronger side coming from the mezcal. A great harmony of flavors. Choose a mezcal with spice and sweet notes, and you will get a fantastic cocktail. And, as the saying goes, a pome (apple) a day keeps the doctor away . . .

YIELD: 5 COCKTAILS

11⅔ ounces or 1½ cup (350 ml) Apple-Infused Mezcal (page 190)

1 cup (200 ml) Apple & Pear Cordial (page 186)

11⅔ ounces or 1½ cup (350 ml) brewed white white cocoa tea, such as T2*

*The first white is for white tea leaves; the second white refers to white cocoa. The combination is unforgettable.

(1) Combine apple-infused mezcal, apple & pear cordial, and white white cocoa tea, such as T2, in a jar.

(2) Pour the liquid into the soda siphon and fill it with CO_2. Store it in the fridge for 1 hour before serving.

(3) Agitate the siphon before using it and pour into a chilled single rocks glass.

Bartender's Tip: *A siphon is a great tool to have at home. You can use it to make sparkling water, but also to prepare unique fizzy cocktails. They will give the right zest to your parties.*

CHAPTER 7:
HOMEMADE
COCKTAIL INGREDIENTS

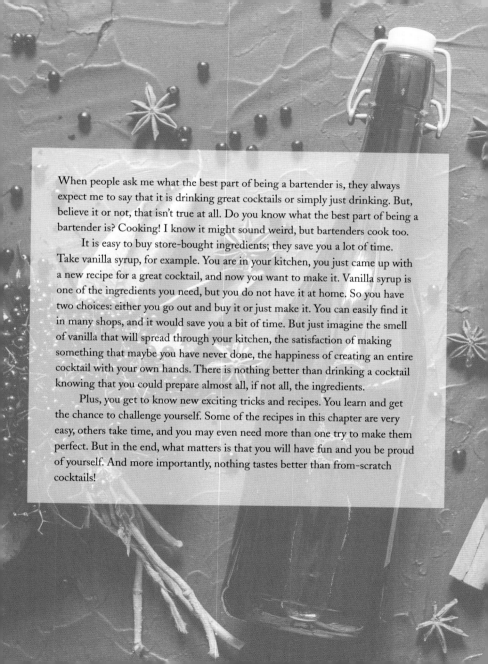

When people ask me what the best part of being a bartender is, they always expect me to say that it is drinking great cocktails or simply just drinking. But, believe it or not, that isn't true at all. Do you know what the best part of being a bartender is? Cooking! I know it might sound weird, but bartenders cook too.

It is easy to buy store-bought ingredients; they save you a lot of time. Take vanilla syrup, for example. You are in your kitchen, you just came up with a new recipe for a great cocktail, and now you want to make it. Vanilla syrup is one of the ingredients you need, but you do not have it at home. So you have two choices: either you go out and buy it or just make it. You can easily find it in many shops, and it would save you a bit of time. But just imagine the smell of vanilla that will spread through your kitchen, the satisfaction of making something that maybe you have never done, the happiness of creating an entire cocktail with your own hands. There is nothing better than drinking a cocktail knowing that you could prepare almost all, if not all, the ingredients.

Plus, you get to know new exciting tricks and recipes. You learn and get the chance to challenge yourself. Some of the recipes in this chapter are very easy, others take time, and you may even need more than one try to make them perfect. But in the end, what matters is that you will have fun and you be proud of yourself. And more importantly, nothing tastes better than from-scratch cocktails!

GARNISHES AND EXTRAS

Garnishes can be pretty challenging, but they can also be so much fun and push your creativity to places you never thought you would go. Everything around you, edible or not, can be a garnish. Just try, experiment, and do not forget to have fun!

CHERRY BLEND

If you want to go the extra mile, you can make your own homemade cherry blend. It is easy to make, and it will be delicious. You can use these liqueur soaked cherries over ice cream or dessert. You can also add them into cocktails, such as the Lady Manhattan, Plumee, Mezcal Fever, and Red Rhuby (pages 146, 78, 91, and 94). Plus, you can use this method to preserve cherries (for example, if you bought too many). Store in a dry and cold place.

YIELD: 2 CUPS (250 GRAMS)

2 cups (250 grams) fresh cherries, stems and pits removed

1 cup (250 ml) sweet vermouth

1 cup (250 ml) Amaro Del Capo

1 cup (200 grams) sugar

1 cup (200 ml) water

(1) Place cherries, sweet vermouth, Amaro Del Capo, sugar, and water into a jar, cover, and store in a cool and dark place for 3 months, stirring daily.

(2) Use or cover, and store at room temperature for up to 1 year.

CHOCOLATE-DIPPED AMARETTI

Chocolate makes everything better. And the secret to smooth dipping chocolate is a few tablespoons of coconut oil—it makes the chocolate harden faster and a little thicker. Use it as a garnish for Sweet Dreams (page 152) or as a small treat!

1 cup (160 grams)
chocolate chips

2 tablespoons (15 ml)
coconut oil

10 amaretti cookies

(1) Melt chocolate chips with coconut oil in a double boiler over medium-high heat or in the microwave, in 30-second intervals, stirring in between, until completely melted.

(2) With tongs, gently dip the bottom of the amaretto into the chocolate and place it upside-down on a baking sheet. Refrigerate until the chocolate is set, at least 30 minutes.

CLEAR PEAR

A clear pear is basically a tiny clear slice of pear dipped in sugar syrup. You can eat clear pears as a crispy candy or use them as a garnish to your cocktails, such as Single Ladies (page 96), and cakes.

YIELD: 8 SLICES

1 pear

1 cup (300 ml)
Simple Syrup 2:1
(page 242)

(1) Preheat the oven to 200°F (93°C). Set out 2 baking sheets, and line them both with a silicone baking mat or parchment paper.

(2) Wash a pear and cut it into around 15 thin slices (1 to 1.5 mm), using a mandoline.

(3) In a saucepan, submerge pear slices in simple syrup 2:1 and cook over medium-high heat until the syrup gets thick and the pear gets clear.

(4) Place clear pear slices on 1 of the lined baking sheets, and then cover them with the other silicone baking mat and baking sheet on top, to prevent them from burning.

(5) Roast in the oven at 200°F (93°C) for 30 minutes.

(6) Let them dry and cool down. Store clear pears in a sealed jar at room temperature for up to 2 days.

CHOCOLATE STAMPS

You can easily buy chocolate in different shapes and sizes, but if you want to have some fun (with your kids especially), then buy silicone stamps. On websites and houseware shops, you can find many of them: fruit shapes, animals, and feathers too. I use a cactus-shaped silicone stamp for the Aphrodisiac Old-Fashioned (page 172), a pig stamp for A Wild Pig (page 133). You can add a feather stamp to the Jimador Soul (page 136). It's amazing how many funny stamps you can find.

Use stamped chocolate to garnish of your drinks or mugs of hot cocoa. They will make your guests smile, and they are delicious.

The process is very easy and you can use any kind of chocolate you like. Indulge yourself in the huge variety of chocolate on the market.

At least 1 bar chocolate

(1) In a bain-marie (a glass bowl set over top a saucepan of gently simmering water), melt a chocolate bar.

(2) Fill the stamp of your choice with melted chocolate and place it in the freezer for 2 hours or until it's solid.

Bartender's Tip: *Melt at least 1 bar of chocolate at a time; smaller amounts can burn too quickly.*

GRAPEFRUIT FOAM

For this recipe, you will need grapefruit, soy lecithin, and a milk frother! It might look complicated, but it is not. And the result will surprise you: a yummy and colorful foam to add as a garnish to your cocktails, such as the Minesweeper Flower (page 112). It is so delicious that everyone will ask for more!

YIELD: ⅔ CUP (150 ML)

⅔ cup (150 ml) freshly squeezed grapefruit juice

1⅔ ounce (50 ml) Simple Syrup 2:1 (page 242)

1 teaspoon (3.5 grams) soy lecithin*

*Soy lecithin smooths out a drink's texture and can also work as a stabilizer. Find it at most health food stores or online.

(1) Squeeze grapefruit and combined the juice in a blender with simple syrup 2:1 and soy lecithin.

(2) Blend it at least 30 seconds, until soy lecithin is dissolved.

(3) Let it rest for 15 minutes.

(4) Use a milk frother to froth the liquid until you get a smooth foam.

(5) With the help of a teaspoon, gently pour into the glass, forming a layer.

MANDARIN FOAM

Mandarin Foam is simply delicious. Once you try it, you will not be able to do without it! Creamy, fresh, and delicate, it is going to be your new temptation. You can use it to garnish your cocktails, such as A Cloudy Mandarin (page 64), or even cupcakes. To be honest, it is pretty tasty on its own.

YIELD: 2 CUPS (400 ML)

---

1 cup (200 ml) mandarin juice (store-bought or freshly squeezed from about 4–5 mandarins)*

½ teaspoon (2 grams) vanilla bean paste

½ cup (100 grams) caster sugar

6 medium egg white*

*Alternatively, you can use 1 teaspoon (2 grams) sucrose esters (a.k.a. sugar esters) for a more stable foam.

(1) Combine mandarin juice, vanilla bean paste, caster sugar, and egg white (or sucrose esters) in a siphon.

(2) Charge it with a cream soda charger. Store in the fridge for at least 1 hour before serving.

(3) After using, store the remainder in the fridge for up to 6 days.

ORANGE ICE

Orange Ice is a creative way to serve sipping drinks. It has a charming color and a citrusy aroma. I love it in a classic Negroni, or in the Smoky Artichoke (page 116), but you can also use it to make a fantastic slushy: Just crush it, add some sugar and a bit of orange juice.

YIELD: ABOUT 4 CUPS

Peel from six oranges (10½ ounces)

4 ¼ cups (1 liter) water

(1) Combine orange peel and water in a medium-sized saucepan over high heat.

(2) Bring to a boil, stir occasionally, and cook for 20 minutes.

(3) Remove from heat and let cool. When cool, strain into a container, either a 6-cube ice tray or a block mold, and discard orange peels.

(4) Freeze for 24 hours. Unmold if using an ice-cube tray or use an ice pick to carve the ice into 6 blocks. Frozen in an airtight container, orange ice lasts up to 3 months.

PARMESAN CHIP

A parmesan chip is crunchy and delicious, and you can use it as a garnish for your drinks, such as Call Your Mama (page 68). Otherwise, you can have it with salads, or it can be a yummy snack, too. It is extremely easy to make but remember to eat it within a few minutes; otherwise, it will lose its crunchiness. (It will still be good, but not as good as a fresh one.)

YIELD: 1 CHIP

¼ **cup (30 grams) grated parmesan**

(1) In a hot skillet over medium-high heat, place grated parmesan in a round disc.

(2) Let it cook for 3 to 5 minutes at medium-high heat. Do not turn it until it is crispy and golden brown adequately cooked; otherwise, it will break.

(3) Flip it with a spatula's help and cook the other side for another 2 to 3 minutes or until it gets crispy and golden brown.

RASPBERRY TUILE

Raspberry tuile are a beautiful way to garnish your cocktails, such as Madre Tierra, and cakes. They are shiny and intense in flavor. You can give the mixture the shape that you like the most; try rolling them around the handle of a wooden spoon or pressing them over an upside-down shot glass to make a flower-like shape. No matter how you shape your bubble, you will have a unique garnish!

YIELD: ABOUT 4 TUILES (DEPENDING ON HOW BIG YOU MAKE THEM)

---

4 cups (600 grams)
fresh raspberries

⅛ (30 grams) cup
caster sugar

(1) Preheat oven to 180°F (80°C). Line a baking sheet with a silicone baking mat or parchment paper.

(2) Purée raspberries and sugar into a blender. Blitz at low speed until smooth and then pass through a sieve or fine-mesh strainer; discard any solids.

(3) Put the mixture back into the blender and blend at maximum speed for 2 minutes more to make it even smoother.

(4) Spoon the mixture onto the lined baking sheet, spreading it out in one large shape.

(5) Bake for 2 hours. Remove and shape quickly—while hot—as you wish.

Bartender's Tip: These tuile are a cocktail garnish, not the classic French cookie by the same name. There are three types of tuile, all made with a similar technique: the French cookies, coral tuile (which is a flour and water garnish), and this raspberry tuile (which is similar to the coral tuile, but without flour). For garnishing cocktails, I prefer this flourless recipe.

SUNFLOWER SEED AND ALMOND PRALINE

This is a delicious and crunchy praline to use as a garnish on your drinks, such as Quiet Chaos (page 92), or on your cakes. And it's perfect on its own, as a small treat. You will love it!

½ cup (100 grams) caster sugar

2 tablespoons (30 ml) water

¼ cup (30 grams) sunflower seeds

¼ (20 grams) almonds

(1) In a saucepan over low heat, combine sugar and water, then cook for 5 minutes, stirring occasionally.

(2) Increase heat to high and bring sugar syrup to a boil. When boiling, let it cook for 5 to 10 minutes without stirring. When the mixture turns golden, remove it from heat and let it rest for 2 minutes.

(3) Stir in sunflower seeds and almonds. Prepare a parchment paper-lined baking sheet and pour the mixture out onto it. Let it cool.

(4) Once cool, break praline into shards. Store praline, layered with a parchment paper in a container with a lid in the fridge for up to 6 days.

CORDIALS

Cordials are amazing ingredients. Not only you can make cocktails in order to give them an extra flavor, but also you can use them for refreshing mocktails. In summer, especially, mix a cordial with sparkling water, and voilà, you get a great drink to enjoy while sunbathing!

APPLE & PEAR CORDIAL

Apples and pears are a good match for making a delicious fruity cordial. You can use it in sour cocktails, such as The Infamous Pome (page 173), as the sweet part of it. If you combine cordial and sparkling wine, you will have an incredible twist of a Mimosa. Mezcal sour with apple & pear cordial is very tasty too. You can use the cordial in soft drinks as well. If you add sparkling water, you can get a refreshing mocktail for kids.

YIELD: ⅔ CUP (150 ML)

---

1 medium granny smith apples

1½ medium Concorde pears

⅝ cup (125 grams) caster sugar

¼ teaspoon (1.5 grams) citric acid powder

(1) Peel apples and pears, halve them, and roast them in the oven at 350°F (180°C) until they turn brown.

(2) Juice roasted apples and pears in a centrifugal juicer.

(3) Combine roasted apple and pear juice with caster sugar and citric acid powder in a saucepan over medium-high heat, and, stirring occasionally, bring it to a boil.

(4) Allow to cool, strain, and bottle. Store it in the fridge for up to 2 weeks.

Bartender's Tip: If you like to use different types of pears and apples, do not forget to adjust the sugar amount according to their sweetness.

CHILI CORDIAL

Sweet and spicy with a hint of citrus, it is very versatile. You can use it in Hot Like Hell (page 130) or many classic cocktails, such as Margaritas and Daiquiris. But you can use it to season your food too. I use Bird's Eye chili because it is medium-spicy and does not overheat the drink. If you like a bit more of fire, you can try to make this cordial with different chilies.

YIELD: CUP (200 ML)

---

1 cup (200 grams) caster sugar

6 medium fresh bird's eye chilies

1 cup (200 ml) water

½ teaspoon (3 grams) citric acid powder

(1) In a saucepan, combine caster sugar, chili, and water.

(2) Bring it to boil over medium-high heat, stir occasionally, and cook it until the sugar is dissolved. Remove from heat and let cool.

(3) Add citric acid powder and stir. Let it sit for 10 minutes, then strain into a bottle. Store in the fridge for up to 3 months.

CUCUMBER CORDIAL

Cucumber Cordial is refreshing and light. It gives cocktails, such as Appeliza (page 66), a nice kick, but it is also good with just some sparkling water. Or you can make a very tasting cucumber lemonade.

17 OUNCES (500 ML)

Peel of 1 cucumber (about 11⅔ ounces)

1/4 teaspoon (1 gram) Maldon sea salt flakes

1 cup caster sugar*

2 cups (500 ml) water

*Caster sugar is also known as very fine granulated sugar or superfine sugar. If you don't have any, you can easily make your own by pulsing granulated sugar in a food processor.

(1) Place cucumber peel, Maldon sea salt flakes, caster sugar, and water into a food processor and blitz until smooth.

(2) Pass it through a cheesecloth or fine-mesh strainer before using or storing.

(3) Refrigerated in an airtight container, it lasts 1 week.

CUCUMBER & CARAWAY CORDIAL

Clear and smooth in flavor, this cordial is terrific for hot summer days. You can mix it with a splash of tonic water or soda water to get a fantastic and refreshing mocktail for you and your kids. Caraway will give a nice, spiced kick to the cordial, therefore to the mocktails and cocktails, such as La Mar (page 90).

YIELD: 1 CUP (200 ML)

Peels from 3 medium-sized cucumbers

1 pinch salt

1 cup (200 ml) water

½ cup (100 grams) caster sugar

1 teaspoon (3 grams) caraway seeds

(1) Place cucumber peels, salt, water, and caster sugar into a blender and blitz until the mixture is smooth.

(2) Pass it through a muslin cloth or fine-mesh strainer, discard any solids, and place the smooth mixture into a saucepan.

(3) Heat the mixture for 10 minutes over medium-high heat, stirring occasionally. Remove from heat.

(4) Stir in caraway seeds; let the mixture rest for 20 minutes.

(5) Strain it into a jar through a muslin cloth. Cover and store in the fridge for up to 1 week.

INFUSIONS

Infusion is one of the oldest techniques but also one of the easiest and simplest. You can infuse almost anything; it is a versatile technique. It is up to you to play with the elements in order to get new flavors. Do not be afraid of mixing flavors and experimenting; you never know what you can get!

APPLE-INFUSED MEZCAL

Apples release fruity notes into mezcal, maintaining the aromas without overpowering them. It is quite easy to make, and it is also versatile. You can infuse apples in other spirits, such as vodka and whisky.

YIELD: 10 OUNCES OR 1¼ CUPS (300 ML)

---

10 ounces or 1¼ cups (300 ml) mezcal

¾ cup (150 grams) dehydrated apples

(1) Combine mezcal, and dehydrated apples in a sous-vide bag and seal it.

(2) Cook for 2 hours at 131°F (55°C) with a sous vide cooker.

(3) Let cool, fine-strain through a coffee filter, and bottle it. Store in the fridge for up to 3 months.

Bartender's Tip: I recommend this method, but if you do not have a sous vide machine, instead you can seal the mezcal-apple mixture in a jar for 24 hours, frequently shaking it.

BACON FAT-WASHED MEZCAL

This is a delicious method for giving extra flavor and bacon aroma to a mezcal. A bacon fat wash is typically done with Bourbon. But a bacon fat wash is quite versatile, and you can use it with many different spirits and cocktails, such as the mezcal for the Wild Pig (page 13).

YIELD: 8¾ OUNCE (250 ML)

---

5 slices of bacon

8¾ ounce (250 ml) mezcal

(1) Cook bacon in a pan over medium-high heat until the fat is melted to a liquid.

(2) Pour the oil from the fat into a jar, discarding the bacon (make a sandwich or a breakfast with it) and combine mezcal.

(3) Let it sit for 4 hours, and then place it in the freezer overnight. The fat will separate from the alcoholic part.

(4) Strain into a bottle through a muslin cloth, discard fat solids, and store bacon-washed mezcal in the fridge for up 2 weeks.

Bartender's Tip: To fat-wash a spirit, you can use any kind of oil (coconut, sesame, extra virgin olive, avocado, peanut, palm), peanut butter, butter, bacon, and duck fat. You can also add herbs, such as rosemary, for extra flavor.

BANANA CHIP-INFUSED MEZCAL

Infusion is a very good technique to get flavor into spirits without changing their color and texture. The more you leave banana chips infused in mezcal, the more intense the banana flavor will be. Try it with Claire Temptation No. 1 (page 144), it will be delicious!

YIELD: 1¼ OR 10 OUNCES (300 ML)

¾ cup (50 grams) banana chips

1¼ or 10 ounces (300 ml) mezcal

(1) Combine banana chips and mezcal in a jar and seal it.

(2) Let it rest at room temperature for 3 days; shake it occasionally.

(3) Strain into a bottle, cover, and store at room temperature for up to 3 months.

BAY LEAF-INFUSED MEZCAL

Bay leaves give a spiced kick, so you can infuse them with many types of spirits and mix bay leaf infusions in all sorts of cocktails. Or you can just sip and taste a bay leaf-mezcal by itself; it is going to be delicious. Bay leaves give fresh and clean notes to the mezcal. It can make a lovely holiday gift too. Try it with the Wishing Leaf (page 168).

YIELD: 1 CUP (200 ML)

---

5 fresh bay leaves

6 ⅔ ounces or 1 cup (200 ml) mezcal

(1) Combine fresh bay leaves and mezcal in a jar and seal it. Let it infuse at room temperature for 1 week.

(2) Strain into a bottle, cover, and store at room temperature for up to 3 months.

Bartender's Tip: You can accelerate the infusion process with a sous vide cooker: Combine bay leaves and mezcal in a vacuum bag, seal, and cook for 30 minutes at 180°F (80°C). Then let the mixture cool down, strain it, and bottle it. Store it in the fridge.

BUTTER-WASHED MEZCAL

Butter gives a bit of texture to mezcal and enhances the structure of the spirit. It brightens the mezcal flavor, leaving a nice viscosity on the palate, letting the mezcal have a long finish. Check out Sweet Dreams and Aphrodisiac Old Fashioned, two lovely recipes made with Butter-Washed Mezcal.

YIELD: MAKES ABOUT 1¼ CUPS (300 ML)

3½ tablespoons (50 grams) unsalted butter

11⅔ ounces (350 ml) mezcal, at room temperature

(1) Melt butter in a medium saucepan over low heat, until butter begins to clarify and most of the milk solids sink to the bottom of the pot, about 10 to 15 minutes.

(2) In a large tub (16 ounces, ½ liter), fine-strain butter through a muslin cloth into room-temperature mezcal and stir to combine.

(3) Keep the mixture at room temperature for 2 hours, stirring every so often, until butter starts to solidify. Seal, and freeze for 12 to 18 hours to separate butter fat from mezcal.

(4) After freezing, fine strain butter-washed mezcal through layered muslin cloth or superbag into a bottle while still cold. Discard solids. Cover butter-washed mezcal and refrigerate for up to 2 weeks.

Bartender's Tip: Note that some of the volume will be lost in the freezing. And temperatures are important: If mezcal is too cold when added to butter, it will cause the butter to split and separate, so be sure to store it at room temperature before use.

CHAMOMILE DRY VERMOUTH

Like all tea infusions, a chamomile vermouth is easy to make. Remember to use mid- to top-shelf spirit to get a high-quality infusion. A nice touch of chamomile to dry vermouth will make it more floral and grassier. Try it out in the Quiet Chaos (page 92).

YIELD: 3⅓ OUNCES (100 ML)

1 teaspoon chamomile flowers (1 gram or 1 bag)

3⅓ ounces (100 ml) dry vermouth

(1) Combine chamomile flowers and dry vermouth in a jar and seal it. Shake to combine, and let it rest for 2 hours.

(2) Strain through a muslin cloth or fine-mesh strainer into a bottle, cover, and store it in the fridge for up to 3 weeks.

CHERRY-INFUSED TEQUILA

Adding cherries to your tequila will give it a nice fruity flavor. Even the color will change slightly, giving a new look to your drinks, such as the Lady Manhattan (page 146). Used alongside Maraschino, Tequila-infused Cherries will bright up the fruitiness of the drink, and the cherry-infused tequila will be more drinkable even to delicate palates.

YIELD: ⅘ CUPS (200 ML)

⅔ cup (100 grams) cherries, washed, stems and pits removed

⅘ cup (200 ml) tequila

(1) Place cherries and tequila into a jar and seal with a lid.

(2) Let it sit for 3 days, occasionally giving it a stir or a gentle shake.

(3) Strain the liquid into a bottle (But do not throw the cherries away! Use them as a garnish of your cocktails or desserts). Store in the fridge for up to 1 month.

CLEMENTINE PEEL-INFUSED MEZCAL

This can be a great gift for Christmas. It's a flavorful sweet and smoky infusion that can be used in cocktails, such as Cleme My Mind (page 162), and, why not, to sip by itself.

YIELD: 6⅔ OUNCES (200 ML)

Peels of 2 clementines, washed before peeling

6⅔ ounces (200 ml) mezcal

(1) Infuse clementine peels with mezcal in a jar. Cover and let rest for 12 hours at room temperature, shaking occasionally.

(2) Strain into a bottle, cover, and store in the fridge for up to 2 weeks.

COFFEE BEAN-INFUSED MEZCAL

If you do not have a sous-vide set up, you can use a saucepan. (See page 52 on sous vide equipment), following the same temperature and cooking time.

In this delicious combination of coffee and mezcal, the beans release a great aroma into the spirit. Use dark roasted beans; the stronger the coffee is, the more pungent the aroma will be. Stick with one variety or a mix of as many different flavored coffee beans as you like. Try it out with A Cloudy Mandarin (page 64); you will love it.

YIELD: 6⅔ OUNCES (200 ML)

6⅔ ounces (200 ml) mezcal

⅓ cup (30 grams) whole coffee beans

(1) Toast coffee beans in a pan over medium heat, stirring occasionally to toast both sides. Remove from heat and let cool.

(2) Pour mezcal into an infusion jar or a vacuum bag.

(3) Add the roasted coffee beans and seal the jar or the bag.

(4) Give it a shake and allow it to sit for 8 hours at room temperature.

(5) Strain the mezcal through a fine strain and bottle it.

(6) Store it in a cold, dry place for 3 months.

Bartender's Tip: If you are hesitant, try a small batch first. Pour a couple of shots of mezcal into a jar and add a handful of coffee beans. Allow this to infuse and see if you like it.

EARL GREY TEA-INFUSED TEQUILA

With this infusion, you will get a darker tequila and more pungent citrusy notes. The more you leave the tea in infusion, the more it will have a stronger and bitter taste. So be careful with the timing. Try it in An Englishman in Oaxaca (page 84).

YIELD: 2 COCKTAILS

---

3 ounces (90 ml) tequila

2 teaspoons (4 grams) loose-leaf Earl Grey tea

(1) Combine tequila and Earl Grey loose-leaf tea in a container and seal it.

(2) Let it infuse for 30 minutes.

(3) Strain the liquid and bottle it. Store it in the fridge for up to 3 months.

EXOTIC DRIED FRUITS-INFUSED MEZCAL

At the market, you can find many different bags of exotic dried fruits. The mix I use for Summer Flute (page 97) is made of dehydrated coconut, dehydrated pineapple, dehydrated banana chips, and dehydrated goji berries. But you can use any dried fruit mix you like. Tropical notes will be added to your mezcal, making it even more delicious.

YIELD: 6⅔ OUNCES (200 ML)

¾ cup (100 grams) exotic dry fruit

6⅔ ounces (200 ml) mezcal

(1) In a jar, combine dried fruit and mezcal.

(2) Seal it and let it rest for 3 days, shaking occasionally.

(3) Strain into a bottle, cover, and store at room temperature for up to 3 weeks.

LEMON, ORANGE, PINK GRAPEFRUIT PEEL-INFUSED MEZCAL

Once you try this infusion, you will not be able to do without it. It starts with a citrus aroma, and then embraces you with flavor. The zesty note of citrus makes mezcal fruitier. Try it out with La Medicina del Jimador (page 97).

YIELD: 6⅔ OUNCES (200 ML)

2 lemons

2 oranges

1 grapefruit

6⅔ ounces (200 ml) mezcal

(1) Wash lemons, oranges, and grapefruit. Peel them and place the peel in a vacuum bag or a jar.

(2) Pour mezcal and seal the bag or jar. Occasionally stir, and let it infuse for six hours at room temperature.

(3) Strain into a bottle, cover, and store it in the fridge for up to three months.

PEPPERMINT DRY VERMOUTH

Peppermint adds a menthol touch to dry vermouth, spicing it up a little bit. Make small batches and give it as a gift. Your friends will love it. It's fantastic in a Mountain Path (page 148) and in classic dry martinis!

YIELD: 6⅔ OUNCES OR 1 CUP (200 ML)

6⅔ ounces or 1 cup (200 ml) dry vermouth

teaspoons (4 grams) loose leaf peppermint tea

(1) Combine dry vermouth and loose leaf peppermint tea in a jar. Cover, and let it infuse for 1 hour, gently stirring or shaking occasionally.

(2) Strain into a bottle, cover, and store in the fridge for up to 3 months.

PISTACHIO BUTTER

Of course, you can buy pistachio butter, but it is very easy to make, and you will be proud of it. You can choose the consistency you like, and it will be a real pleasure at first taste. You can use it in cocktails, such as A Jimador Soul (page 136), on your sandwiches, cakes, or ice cream! But I am sure you can find as many uses as you want.

YIELD: 2 CUPS (250 GRAMS)

3½ cups (430 grams) unsalted raw shelled pistachios

2 tablespoons (20 grams) Maldon sea salt flakes

1 tablespoon (20 grams) agave nectar

(1) Roast pistachios in an oven at 328°F (165°C) for 10 minutes, rotating the pans halfway through the roasting time. Let cool.

(2) Place roasted pistachios, Maldon sea salt flakes, and agave into a blender or food processor and blend them, starting from a low speed (about 30 seconds to 1 minute) and then increase speed and blend for about 3 to 4 minutes until you get a smooth and creamy butter. Choose your consistency and be careful, because the longer you mix, the softer it will be.

(3) Store, covered, in a glass jar in the fridge for up to 1 month or in a freezer for up to 3 months.

PISTACHIO BUTTER-WASHED MEZCAL

Pistachio Butter-Washed Mezcal made with a sous-vide will release better the pistachio's flavor into the mezcal. If you do not have a sous vide cooker, you can use a saucepan, following the same temperature and cooking time. This process can be done with any nuts. Try it with A Jimador Soul and a Pistachio Sour (page 136 and 150).

YIELD: 2 COCKTAILS

---

2 cups (500 ml) mezcal

¼ cup (60 grams) Homemade Pistachio Butter (page 203)

(1) Place mezcal and homemade pistachio butter in a vacuum bag and seal it.

(2) Place the bag in a sous-vide for three hours at 131°F (55°C).

(3) Let it cool down and strain into a bottle, cover, and store at room temperature for up to 2 weeks.

Bartender's Tip: When you strain the pistachio butter-washed mezcal into the jar, you will get some nutty, mezcal soaked leftovers, and with them, you can make some fantastic desserts.

SICHUAN PEPPERCORN-INFUSED MEZCAL

When you infuse Sichuan peppercorn into mezcal, the latter gets a stronger flavor. So, first, you will taste the smokiness of the spirit, then an incredible peppery long finish. You will be amazed by the unique flavor of the infusion and Black Sunset (page 86) will be delicious with it. The more you allow the peppercorn to sit, the stronger its flavor will be. So do not leave it for too long.

YIELD: 3⅓ OUNCE (100 ML)

3⅓ ounce (100 ml) mezcal

2 teaspoons (5 grams) whole Sichuan peppercorn

(1) Combine mezcal and Sichuan peppercorn into a jar and seal it. Store it at room temperature for 3 hours.

(2) Strain the liquid into a bottle, and it is ready for use. Store it at room temperature for up to 3 months.

RASPBERRIES CHARTREUSE

Yellow Chartreuse is a sweet, spiced liqueur. It is a lighter variation of Green Chartreuse, with a strong taste of herbs and plants. It pairs well with the acidity of raspberries, and together they deliver a sensational flavor. Try in a Madre Tierra (page 72).

YIELD: 6⅔ OUNCES (200 ML)

6⅔ ounces (200 ml) Yellow Chartreuse

10 fresh raspberries, washed and sliced in half

(1) Seal raspberries in a zip-top plastic bag.

(2) Place it in a sous vide at 130°F (55°C) for 2 hours.

(3) Remove and let cool. Strain, bottle, and store in the fridge for up to 1 month.

STAR ANISE-INFUSED MEZCAL

A strong anise flavor will give character to your mezcal, adding a signature touch to your cocktails, such as A Tropical Winter (page 122). It's a warm infusion with a winter recall that you can combine with tropical fruits.

YIELD: 1¼ CUP OR 10 OUNCES (300 ML)

1¼ cup or 10 ounces
(300 ml) mezcal

6 star anises

(1) Combine star anise and mezcal in a jar and seal it.

(2) Let it infuse for 24 hours, occasionally stirring gently.

(3) Strain the liquid into a bottle, cover, and store at room temperature for up to 3 months.

THREE PEPPERCORN-INFUSED MEZCAL

Each peppercorn gives a unique flavor to mezcal, but don't go overboard; they can drastically change the flavor of a drink. That said, do not be worry about using this infusion in your cocktails because there is a vast range of drinks that you can make with it, such as the Back to Smoke (page 158), a twist of Basil Smash (replace gin with Three Peppercorn-Infused Mezcal), and a Dark & Stormy (substitute dark rum with Three Peppercorn-Infused Mezcal).

YIELD: 6⅔ OUNCES (200 ML)

6⅔ ounces (200 ml) mezcal

⅙ teaspoon (0.5 gram) ground Sichuan peppercorn

½ teaspoon (1 gram) ground pink peppercorn

½ teaspoon (1 gram) ground black peppercorn

(1) Combine mezcal, ground Sichuan peppercorn, ground pink peppercorn, and ground black peppercorn in a jar at room temperature for 4 hours.

(2) Fine strain through a muslin cloth into a bottle that has a lid. Cover and store in the fridge for up to 3 weeks.

REDUCTIONS

Reduction is all about reducing a quantity of a liquid to amplify the flavors, making the result thicker so that even the cocktail will have more body and texture.

WHITE ALE REDUCTION

Reduction gets the most flavor out of beers; added to cocktails, it makes them rich and with a good body. Blanche Denamur has spiced, herbal notes, with a hint of lemon, making it a good match for Mountain Path (page 148).

YIELD: 1 CUP (200 ML)

½ pint (200 ml) white ale, such as Blache Denamur

1 cup (200 grams) caster sugar

(1) In a saucepan, combine white ale, such as Blanche Denamur, and caster sugar.

(2) Cook it at medium heat, stir occasionally, until sugar is dissolved.

(3) Let it cool down and strain into a bottle. Cover and store it in the fridge for up to 1 week.

SODAS

Add CO_2 to a liquid, making it fizzy, and you have a soda. In this way, you also compress all the flavor, increasing the freshness and aroma in a drink.

HOMEMADE GINGER BEER

Ginger beer is very easy to buy, but homemade ginger beer is next level. You can genuinely taste the real, fresh essence of ginger, which will spice up your cocktails. It is fantastic in the Spicy, Tiger! (page 80). A heads-up: You are going to need a soda syphon to get beautiful bubbles. Homemade ginger beer has a 3-week shelf life.

YIELD: 2½ CUPS (20 OUNCES)

15¼ inches fresh ginger, peeled and cut into ½-inch pieces

1 medium lemon, sliced in half

⅘ cups (187.5 grams) caster sugar

11 dashes (3 ml) Angostura bitters

4 ¼ cups (1 liter) still water

(1) Combine ginger, lemon halves, caster sugar, Angostura bitters, and water in a medium saucepan over high heat. Cover and bring to boil.

(2) Reduce heat, leave covered, and simmer on low heat for 2 hours, gently stirring occasionally.

(3) Pass through cheesecloth or a fine-mesh sieve, bottle, and refrigerate. When cool, pour into a soda syphon, close it, and insert a CO_2 charge.

(4) Shake the syphon, and it's ready to use.

Variation: Virgin Moscow Mule

Homemade Ginger Beer is so good by itself. Or you can mix it (¾ cup–25 ml) with lime (2 tablespoons freshly squeezed), soda water (¼ cup–7.5 ml), mint leaves (4 leaves) and crushed ice to get a refreshing Virgin Moscow Mule.

LAPSANG SOUCHONG TEA SODA

A fizzy tea infusion that will make any of your drinks delightful, such as Black Sunset (page 86). The smoky, cedar, and pine notes of the tea are more enhanced in a sparkling solution, giving a refreshing taste to cocktails.

YIELD: 2 CUPS (500 ML)

---

2 teaspoon (4 grams) loose-leaf Lapsang souchong tea

2 cups (500 ml) water

1 cup (200 grams) caster sugar

(1) Combine Lapsang souchong loose leaf tea and water in a saucepan and bring it to boil.

(2) Add caster sugar, stir occasionally, and let it cook until the sugar is dissolved. Remove from heat and let it cool.

(3) Strain tea mixture into the siphon and charge it with CO_2. Store the charged siphon in the fridge for 1 hour before using it because both the liquid and the siphon need to be cold to allow for carbonation. You can use it all at once or store it in the fridge for up to 6 days.

SOLUTIONS

In addition to balancing a cocktail's flavors, acid solutions are a great sustainable alternative because they give your cocktail a longer shelf-life. Done right, they also offer consistency to your cocktail so that it will always have the same flavor. (When you use fresh citrus, a cocktail will always have a slightly different taste.)

CITRIC ACID SOLUTION 10%

This solution is an excellent way to amplify cocktails made with fresh juice. Your drinks, such as the Posy and Claire Temptation No. 1 (pages 131 and 144), will be more refreshing too. The percentage refers to the proportion of citric acid in the water.

YIELD: ½ CUP (100 ML)

½ cup (100 ml) water

2 teaspoons (10 grams) citric acid powder

(1) Combine water and citric acid powder in a jar and stir it until the powder is dissolved.

(2) Bottle it, and it is ready to use. Cover and store in the fridge for up to 1 month.

MALIC SOLUTION 10%

Malic is found in fruits and wine. In cocktails, such as Claire Temptation No. 1 (page 144), it is used to give a similar tartness of green apple.

YIELD: ½ CUP (100 ML)

---

2 teaspoons (10 grams) malic acid powder

½ cup (100 ml) water

(1) In a jar, combine malic acid powder and water.

(2) Stir until malic acid powder is dissolved.

(3) Strain it into a bottle, cover, and store in the fridge for up to 2 weeks.

SALINE SOLUTION 10%

Here's a solution to enhance the sweet components of the cocktails, such as the Corn Flip (page 143). It helps to reduce bitterness as well.

YIELD: 1 CUP (200 ML)

---

1 cup (200 ml) water

2 tablespoon (20 grams) Maldon sea salt flakes

(1) Boil water for 20 minutes to remove any impurities. Remove from heat and let cool.

(2) Combine boiled and cooled water with Maldon sea salt flakes in a jar; stir until the salt is dissolved.

(3) Bottle it, and it is ready to use. Store in the fridge for up to 1 week.

TARTARIC AND MALIC SOLUTION 6%

This is a water solution that balances a cocktail and adds a bit of acidity to the final product. Tartaric is an organic acid that develops naturally during the fermentation and it is found in fruits (such as grapes and citrus). When used it in wine or cocktails, it acts as a preservative. Malic acid is an organic compound that occurs in fruits, vegetables and wines. It is used to give a tart flavor. So, keep in mind that if you use this solution, you do not have to add any other acidic part to the cocktails. You can find these ingredients in spice shops and online. Use Tartaric and Malic Solution 6% in the Plumee (page 78) as the acidic part of the cocktail.

YIELD: 1 CUP AND 2 TEASPOONS (250 ML)

1½ teaspoons (7.5 grams) cream of tartar (a.k.a. tartaric acid powder)

1 cup plus 2 teaspoons (250 ml) water

1½ teaspoons (7.5 grams) malic acid powder

(1) Combine cream of tartar and water in a saucepan over medium-high heat, stirring occasionally, and bring to a boil.

(2) Once boiling, remove from heat and let cool.

(3) Pour the cooled cream of tartar solution and malic acid powder into a bottle together, cover, and shake. Store at room temperature for up to 1 month.

Bartender's Tip: *Using boiling water to make this solution gives it a longer shelf-life.*

SYRUPS AND MORE

Mixers help deliver flavors. There is a world of varieties of syrups, juices, sorbet, and purees. They are easy to make, and they are very versatile, meaning there are a lot of recipes where you can use them. Plus, making your own mixers can be a smart way to reduce waste at home. (Leftover apple? Make an apple syrup!)

APPLE SYRUP

A fantastic syrup that will give you the feeling of eating an apple pie! You can use it for a sweet part of a classic Gimlet, for a Candy Fizz (page 88), or you can add it to your mocktails, too.

YIELD: 1 CUP (250 ML)

---

1 whole green apple, peeled and chopped into small pieces

2 whole lemons, chopped into small pieces

6 ⅔ ounces (200 ml) Simple Syrup 2:1 (page 242)

1¼ cups (300 ml) water

(1) In a saucepan over medium-high heat, mix apples and lemons (peel and flesh) with simple syrup and water.

(2) Bring it to boil and continue to cook it for 10 minutes at medium-high heat, stirring occasionally. Remove from heat and let it rest for one hour.

(3) Strain into a bottle, cover, and store it in the fridge for up to 3 weeks.

AGAVE WATER (2:1)

When it's made into a syrup, agave gets less thick, making it is easier to mix and balance with other cocktail ingredients. Agave nectar is quite sweet; to cut the sweetness and balance a cocktail—such as a Pink Julep (page 109)—you can make this dilution with water.

YIELD: ½ CUP (130 ML)

⅓ cup (100 grams) agave nectar

⅓ cup (50 ml) hot water

(1) Place agave nectar and hot water in a jar and mix until they are well combined, the mixture is smooth, and the agave nectar is dissolved.

(2) Let it cool down and strain into a bottle. Store it in the fridge for up to 3 months.

AVOCADO PIT ORGEAT

Orgeat is an almond syrup, and it is used a lot to give flavor to cocktails. Similarly, the avocado pit orgeat is avocado pit syrup and is a sustainable way to make orgeat. I like it very much, not only because it has a lovely, toasted flavor, but also because it is a perfect example of how you can use waste to make something new and delicious. You can substitute Almond orgeat with Avocado Pit Orgeat in many classic cocktails. Mai Tai, Trinidad Sour, and Army & Navy will be fantastic. Besides cocktails, such as Spicy, Tiger!(page 80), you can use it in cakes as well. You won't find a recipe with this kind of orgeat, but you can substitute almond syrup with avocado pit orgeat, for example.

MAKES 2½ CUPS (600 ML)

---

2 or 3 avocado pits, scrubbed to remove oil and flesh

1⅔ cup (400 grams) caster sugar

1⅔ cup (400 ml) water

(1) Roast avocado pits on a baking sheet in a convection oven at 325°F oven at 350°F for 90 minutes.

(2) Turn oven up to 375°F (190°C) convection or 400°F (200°C) conventional, and roast for another 15 minutes. Let cool, then roughly chop the roasted pits into small pieces.

(3) In a saucepan over high heat, combine roasted avocado pits with sugar and water; boil for 10 minutes. Remove from heat and let cool.

(4) Put into a blender, and blend until smooth. (If you have a thermomix, do not chop the roasted pits; instead mix them with sugar and water straight into the thermomix for 2 minutes at setting 7.)

(5) Pass through cheesecloth or a fine-mesh sieve, and bottle for use. Store in an airtight bottle or jar in the refrigerator for up to 3 weeks.

BASIL AND JASMINE TEA SYRUP

This is a sweet syrup with herbal notes. It is very versatile. You can drink it as a mocktail, and it will be very refreshing, or you can add it to your cocktails, such as Madre Tierra (page 72), to give them a special touch.

YIELD: 1⅓ CUPS (300 ML)

---

5 tablespoons (10 grams) jasmine tea

7 fresh basil leaves (or 2 tablespoons dry basil; fresh is preferred.)

1¼ cups (250 grams) caster sugar

1⅓ cups (300 ml) water

(1) Bring water to a boil over high heat.

(2) Remove from heat and combine boiling water with tea and basil.

(3) Let it steep for 10 minutes. Then stir in sugar until it is dissolved.

(4) Cool and strain into a bottle. Cover and store in the fridge for up to 3 months.

More to Try: Here's another use for Basil and Jasmine Tea Syrup. To make a Flora Gimlet: In a shaker, combine 2 ounces (60 ml) gin, 1 ounce (30 ml) lime juice, and ½ ounce (15 ml) basil and jasmine tea syrup. Fill with ice, give it a hard shake, and strain into a coupette. It will be refreshing and a nice alternative to a classic Gimlet.

CABBAGE & NUTMEG SHRUB

A shrub is a combination of water, fruits (or other botanicals, too), sugar, and vinegar, and it is used to give more acidity and complexity to a cocktail. Cabbage & Nutmeg Shrub is a sweet solution with an aftertaste of vinegar. I prefer to use apple cider vinegar because it softens the shrub, making it more delicate. You can also use white vinegar (but in a smaller quantity, adapted to your taste). Try it in the Cab & Meg (page 126).

MAKES 1½ CUP (350 ML)

2 cups (175 grams) cabbage, washed and cut into tiny pieces

1⅔ cup (250 ml) apple cider vinegar

¼ cup (50 grams) caster sugar

½ cup (100 ml) water

½ dessert spoon (2.5 grams) ground nutmeg

(1) Combine cabbage, apple cider vinegar, caster sugar, water, and ground nutmeg in a vacuum bag. Seal it and sous vide for 3 hours at 150°F (65°C).

(2) Fine-strain and bottle. Store in the fridge for up to 3 months.

Bartender's Tip: *If you do not have a sous vide machine, simply cook it in a saucepan, following the same degrees and cooking time.*

CAULIFLOWER JELLY SYRUP

With its nutty, slightly sweet notes, cauliflower works well in this syrup because each of the ingredients has a strong and unique flavor that, combined, will taste amazing. It has sweet, savory, and peppery flavors all together. It is a triumph of flavor in your mouth, a must-try. It is great in Call Me Flower (page 128).

YIELD: 6⅔ OUNCES (200 ML)

1 teaspoon black sesame seeds

1½ cups (150 grams) cauliflower, finely chopped

4 tablespoons (60 ml) apple cider vinegar

3 tablespoons (50 ml) honey

½ cup (125 ml) water

2 pinches black pepper

5 dashes orange bitters

(1) Toast black sesame seeds in a dry pan over high heat for about 2 minutes, stirring occasionally.

(2) Combine cauliflower, apple cider vinegar, honey, water, roasted black sesame seeds, black pepper, and orange bitters in a saucepan.

(3) Bring it to simmer over medium-high heat, and continue to simmer for 10 minutes, stirring occasionally.

(4) Remove from heat and blend the mixture in a blender until it gets smooth.

(5) Strain into a bottle and store it in the fridge for up to 2 weeks.

CINNAMON & CLOVES SYRUP

A Christmassy winter syrup, Cinnamon & Cloves Syrup is almost like drinking a Panettone! Full of spices and flavors, it is excellent in classic cocktails, like Eggnog, as well as flip-style cocktails, like the Mezcal Flip (page 164). You can use it in desserts too. It will be fantastic.

MAKES 1¼ CUPS (300 ML)

3 cinnamon sticks

1 tablespoon whole cloves

1¼ cups (300 ml) water

1½ cups (300 grams) caster sugar

(1) Combine cinnamon sticks, whole cloves, water, and caster sugar in a saucepan.

(2) Cook over medium-high heat it until the sugar is dissolved; remove the saucepan from heat when the mixture starts to boil.

(3) Stir and strain into a bottle.

(4) Cover and store in the fridge for up to 3 months.

CITRUS PEEL SYRUP

Citrus Peel Syrup is a sweet and zesty syrup that can be used in many cocktails, such as the Wild Pig (page 133) and a classic Gin Ricky. Use it instead of simple syrup to add extra flavor. The good thing about this recipe is that you do not have to throw out citrus peel anymore when, for example, you squeeze a fresh orange juice for your breakfast.

YIELD: 1 CUP (200 ML)

Peel of 2 lemons

Peel of 2 oranges

Peel of 2 grapefruits

1 cup (200 grams) caster sugar

1 cup (200 ml) water

¼ teaspoon (1.5 grams) citric acid powder

(1) Put citrus peels into a saucepan.

(2) Cover with sugar and water and bring to a boil over high heat. Cook for 20 minutes at high heat, stirring occasionally.

(3) Remove from heat and combine with citric acid powder. Stir until dissolved. Let it rest for 20 minutes.

(4) Strain into a bottle, cover, and store in the fridge for up to 2 weeks.

CLEAR BANANA SYRUP

Banana syrup is very easy to make, and it gives cocktails a real and full banana flavor that is not that easy to find on the market. Use it in your puddings, waffles, and mocktails, but also cocktails, such as Claire Temptation No. 1, and A Tropical Winter (pages 122 and 144).

MAKES 1 CUP (200 ML)

---

1 cup (200 grams) caster sugar

cup (200 ml) water

1 banana, peeled and cut into small pieces

(1) Cook caster sugar and water in a small saucepan over medium heat, stirring occasionally, for about 10 minutes or until caster sugar is dissolved.

(2) Add banana pieces and cook for 10 minutes more.

(3) Remove from heat and let rest for 20 minutes at room temperature.

(4) Strain into a bottle, and store in the fridge for up to 2 weeks (but check it before throwing it away because it may last longer).

COCONUT SORBET

Sometimes it can be difficult to find coconut sorbet in a store, but do you know what it is easy? Making your homemade coconut sorbet! A refreshing and delicious sorbet that you can add to cocktails, such as A Midday Affair (page 138), and mocktails, it's also delicious eaten with a spoon whenever you would like to have a small treat during a long hot day. Eating it between two courses will clean and refresh your palate as well.

YIELD: 3 SERVES

---

1 cup and 2 teaspoons (250 ml) water

½ cup (100 grams) caster sugar

¾ cup (175 ml) coconut milk

*Buy coconut milk 100%. The thicker it is, the better your sorbet will be.

(1) In a bowl, combine water and sugar.

(2) Mix until sugar is dissolved and add coconut milk.

(3) Mix it well until you get a smooth texture.

(4) Place it in a freezer for 3 hours, taking it out and mixing every 30 minutes.

(5) Keep it in the freezer for at least 2 hours before using it.

DEMERARA SUGAR SYRUP

This is a richer and more flavored sugar syrup that adds caramel and toffee notes and roasted layers to cocktails, such as An Ocean Between Us (page 124).

YIELD: ½ CUP (100 ML)

½ cup (100 ml) boiling hot water

1 cup (200 grams) demerara sugar

(1) In a jar, combine hot water and Demerara sugar.

(2) Mix until sugar is dissolved.

(3) Let it cool down and bottle it.

(4) Store it in the fridge for up to 1 month.

GINGER SYRUP

Ginger Syrup is a must-have in any kitchen. You can use it in many different ways. For example, you can pour it into nice small bottles and give them as a Christmas gift, or you can freeze it in an ice cube tray and use the cubes to make iced tea or lemonade, and you can use it to enrich your meals and cocktails, such as Spicy Spritzo (page 114).

To make a ginger syrup, follow the recipe for Ginger Juice (page 232), and start from there.

YIELD: 6⅔ OUNCES (200 ML)

6⅔ ounces (200 ml) ginger juice (page 232)

1 cup (200 grams) caster sugar

(1) Combine ginger juice and caster sugar in a saucepan over medium-high heat, stirring until caster sugar is dissolved.

(2) Strain into a bottle, cover, and store in the fridge for up to 2 weeks.

GRAPEFRUIT AND PEYCHAUD SYRUP

This syrup has a sweet and tangy kick, and it is delicious with many things, such as ice creams, seafood, and cocktails, such as Quiet Chaos (page 92).

YIELD: 1½ CUP (350 ML)

½ pink grapefruit, washed

1¼ cups (250 grams) caster sugar

1 cup plus 2 teaspoons (250 ml) water

1 ounce (30 ml) Peychaud's Bitters

⅛ teaspoon (0.5 gram) citric acid powder

(1) Slice grapefruits in half and juice them.

(2) In a vacuum bag, combine flesh, juice, caster sugar, water, Peychaud's Bitters, and citric acid powder.

(3) Seal it and put it in a sous vide cooker at 130°F (55°C) for two hours. If you do not have a sous vide machine, simply use a saucepan and follow the same temperature and cooking time.

(4) Strain into a bottle, cover, and store in the fridge for up to 6 days.

GRAPEFRUIT SHERBET

This grapefruit sherbet is an elegant syrup recipe with bright citrus notes; it will be great in the Forbidden Paradise (page 108).

YIELD: ½ CUP (120 ML)

---

2 pink grapefruit peels, white pith removed

¾ cup (150 grams) caster sugar

½ cup (120 ml) freshly squeezed grapefruit juice (strained to remove pulp)

(1) In a small bowl, combine pink grapefruit peel and caster sugar, and muddle them.

(2) Leave it until sugar is dissolved, stirring occasionally. After a while, you will get a kind of oil from the peel; that's the part to use in this recipe. After oil appears, remove and discard peel.

(3) Combine the sugared oil obtained with freshly squeezed grapefruit juice in a jar, seal it, and shake well.

(4) Submerge the jar into a saucepan filled with water and let it boil over high heat for 20 minutes.

(5) Remove from heat and let cool.

(6) Strain into a bottle, cover, and store in the fridge for up to 2 weeks.

Bartender's Tip: Do not mistake this for grapefruit sorbet; they are very different. Sorbet is a frozen dessert made with water, sugar, and fruits. Sherbet, in the United States, is a sorbet with the addition of milk. In the United Kingdom, however, sherbet can be either a sweet powder to add to your drink or, as in this case, a syrup made with sugar, fruit peels, and juice.

GRENADINE

Grenadine is a brilliant red pomegranate syrup. It is sweet and tart, and you can use it in many recipes or substitute it in place of simple syrup. Use it for an El Presidente cocktail or a Shirley Temple mocktail.

YIELD: 1 CUP (200 ML)

---

1 cup (200 ml) pomegranate juice

1 cup (200 gr) caster sugar

(1) In a saucepan over medium heat, combine pomegranate juice and caster sugar. Bring it to a slow boil and constantly stir until sugar is dissolved.

(2) Reduce the heat and cover the saucepan with a lid. Simmer for 15 to 20 minutes, stirring occasionally.

(3) Remove from heat and let cool. Strain into a bottle. Store it in the fridge for up to 2 months.

GRILLED PINEAPPLE SYRUP 1:1

Sweet and fruity, grilled pineapple syrup can be a star in your drinks, such as Fruity Nest (page 70). The light smoky syrup will brighten cocktails and give them a whole new level. You can use it just by itself, adding a dash of lime and sparkling water to make a mocktail. It is even better when you grill the pineapple on a proper grill outside to get the most out of the woody and smoky flavor. You can use it on ice cream and to prepare delicious cakes too.

YIELD: 1 CUP AND 2 TEASPOONS (250 ML)

2½ cups (200 grams) chopped pineapple

About 200 grams caster sugar (depending on the weight of your roasted pineapple juice)

(1) Peel and cut a pineapple in 3–4 inches thick wheels.

(2) Place them on the grill grates of the oven at 350°F (180° C) for 5–10 minutes per side.

(3) Let them cool and place them in a juicer to extract the juice and strain it through a muslin cloth into a jar.

(4) Weigh the juice and combine it with an equal amount of sugar.

(5) Blend it until the sugar is dissolved and the juice is smooth. Strain into a bottle and store it in the fridge for up to 1 week.

Bartender's Tip: *If you want a bit of acidity and a longer shelf-life, mix ¼ teaspoon (1.5 grams) citric acid powder to the juice and the sugar into the blender. The shelf-life will be 2 weeks.*

If you do not have a juicer, place the grilled pineapple slices directly into a blender and blend them at high speed until you get a smooth juice. Then proceed with the other steps.

GINGER JUICE

Use ginger juice for La Medicina del Jimador, Spicy Spritzo, and Quiet Chaos (pages 71, 114, and 92).

YIELD: ⅔ CUP (150 ML)

---

2 cups (200 grams) ginger root, about ½–1-inch piece

(1) Wash and dry ginger root, removing the bruised parts (otherwise, you can peel it, if you prefer).

(2) Cut the roots in small chunks and place them in a blender.

(3) Blend it for 2 minutes or until you get a pasty pulp.

(4) Strain the liquid through a muslin cloth into a jar or bottle and cover it. Store in the fridge for up to 2 weeks.

Bartender's Tip: *You can also add 1 cup (200 ml) water to the blender if you want a lighter ginger punch.*

HOMEMADE VANILLA SYRUP

A delicate and sweet syrup, this recipe will save your money. It is very easy to make and is very versatile, so that you can use it in many cocktails, such as Yellow (page 170). Plus, you can add it to your desserts too.

YIELD: 2 CUPS (500 ML)

---

2 cups (500 ml) water

2½ cups (500 grams) caster sugar

1 teaspoon (4 grams) vanilla extract

(1) In a saucepan over medium heat, combine water and sugar and cook, stirring occasionally, for 10 minutes or until the sugar is dissolved. Remove from heat, let cool, and then stir in vanilla extract.

(2) Strain into a bottle, cover, and it is ready to use or store in a cold, dry place for up to about 3 months, if not longer.

HONEY AND GINGER SYRUP 1:3

A spiced sweet syrup that you can use for La Medicina del Jimador (page 71) and many classic cocktails, such as Penicillin. Add it to your teas and mocktails as well. The syrup will level them up.

YIELD: 1 CUP (200 ML)

⅔ cup (150 ml) ginger juice

⅓ cup (100 gr) honey

Combine ginger juice and honey in a jar and mix until honey is dissolved. The syrup is now ready, and you can use it for making cocktails.

HONEY WATER 2:1

This is a light version of honey, smooth and less sweet. You can use it in your mocktails and cocktails, such as Mezcal Fever (page 91), but teas too. You can pour it into an ice cube tray, freeze it, and then add it to your drinks to sweeten and refreshing them.

YIELD: 6 ⅔ OUNCES (200 ML)

⅔ cup (200 ml) honey

½ cup (100 ml) boiling hot water

(1) In a jar, combine honey and hot water.

(2) Stir until it gets smooth and well mixed.

(3) Strain it through a muslin cloth into a bottle, cover, and store it in the fridge for up to 1 month.

LAPSANG SOUCHONG SYRUP 2:1

A spiced tea that makes an intense syrup. It is very easy to make but be careful about the timing infusion. Do not let it rest for too long; otherwise, you will get a bitter syrup. Plus, the quality of tea is important. If you choose a high-quality tea, you will get a more flavorful syrup. Try it in Back to Smoke (page 158).

YIELD: ½ CUP (125 ML)

½ cup (125 ml) water

½ teaspoon (1 gram) lapsang souchong tea loose leaves

1¼ cups (250 grams) caster sugar

(1) In a saucepan bring water to a boil; remove from heat and add loose lapsang souchong tea leaves.

(2) Let it infuse for 3 to 5 minutes.

(3) Strain it into a jar and stir in caster sugar.

(4) Stir until sugar is dissolved. Bottle it and store it in the fridge for up to 3 weeks.

MARSHMALLOW SYRUP

This is a thick and sweet syrup to add to your cocktails, such as Candy Fizz (page 88), or mocktails. Do not go overboard with the quantity because it is quite sweet.

YIELD: 6⅔ OUNCES (200 ML)

---

5 regular (30 grams) marshmallows

6 ⅔ ounces (200 ml) Simple Syrup 2:1 (page 242)

(1) Combine marshmallows and simple syrup 2:1 in a vacuum bag.

(2) Cook it with a sous vide cooker at 130°F (55°C) for 3 hours.

(3) Strain through a muslin cloth (and keep marshmallows and foam from falling) into a bottle.

(4) Store in the fridge for up to 1 week.

Bartender's Tip: A sous vide cooker is great for making top-notch cocktail ingredients. If you do not have one, you can use a saucepan, following the same temperature and cooking time.

PINK PEPPERCORN
AND AGAVE SYRUP

Pink peppercorn makes agave pungent and gives a warm and peppery aftertaste. The spiciness will vary, depending on how finely the peppercorns are cracked; a finer crack will provide more heat. Be careful, if you have a nut allergy, pink peppercorn may be dangerous for you, as it belongs to the cashew and mango family. Try this syrup in Aga & Peppe (page 156).

YIELD: 1 CUP AND 2 TEASPOONS (250 ML)

⅔ cup (200 grams) agave nectar

1 teaspoon (2 grams) ground pink peppercorn

⅓ cup (65 ml) water

(1) Place agave nectar, ground pink peppercorn, and water in a vacuum bag and seal it.

(2) Cook it with a sous vide cooker at 140°F (60°C) for 2 hours; if you do not have a sous vide machine, use a saucepan instead, and follow the same temperature and cooking time.

(3) Strain into a bottle, cover, and store in the fridge for up 1 month.

POPCORN SYRUP

Popcorn syrup is sweet and yummy. You can prepare it with caramel popcorn, butter popcorn, or salted popcorn. Keep in mind that, in each case, the flavor will be slightly different. It is really up to your taste. I recommend unsalted popcorn for a more natural flavor. Try Popcorn Syrup in the Corn Flip (page 143); you will not be disappointed.

YIELD: ½ CUP (100 ML)

---

6 cups (50 grams) unsalted popped popcorn

½ cup (100 grams) caster sugar

½ cup (100 ml) water

(1) In a saucepan over medium-high heat, combine unsalted popped popcorn, caster sugar, and water.

(2) Bring to a boil, stirring occasionally. Cook until the sugar is dissolved.

(3) Strain through a muslin cloth into a bottle, cover, and store in the fridge for up to 2 weeks.

RASPBERRY SYRUP

Raspberry Syrup is not only delicious but also incredibly versatile. You can use it in cocktails, such as the Berrykilla Julep (page 65) and mocktails, and on treats like ice cream and pancakes too!

YIELD: 1 CUP (200 ML)

1½ cups (150 grams) raspberries

1 cup (200 ml) water

1 cup (200 grams) caster sugar

(1) Combine raspberries with water and caster sugar in a saucepan over medium heat, stirring occasionally; bring to a boil or until the sugar is dissolved. (The longer you simmer, the thicker the syrup will be.) Remove from heat and let it cool down.

(2) Strain the liquid into a bottle. Cover and store in the fridge for up to 3 weeks.

SAMPHIRE OLEO SACCHARUM

"Oleo saccharum" means sugared oil; it's a method used to extract citrus oils from their skin, saving instead of wasting it. Samphire oleo saccharum is a killer combo of the sweetness of the citrus oil and the saltiness of the samphire. Use it in cocktails like the Southside or Samphire Collins (page 132).

YIELD: 1 CUP (200 ML)

---

3 (25 grams) lime zest (all pith removed)

½ cup (100 grams) caster sugar

¾ ounce (25 grams) samphire

¼ cup (50 ml) water

1 teaspoon (2.5 grams) Maldon sea salt flakes

(1) Combine lime zest and caster sugar in a bag, vacuum seal, and put in the fridge overnight.

(2) The next day, in a blender, combine samphire, water, and Maldon sea salt flakes, and blend them at full speed for 30 seconds, until you get a smooth syrup.

(3) Scoop the oleo (the sugared oil) out of the lime zest sugar. In a jar, combine the oleo (the sugared oil) from the lime zest and the samphire mixture from the blender.

(4) Stir well, and strain into a bottle. Store it in the fridge for up to 1 month.

SIMPLE SYRUP 2:1

You can buy simple syrup at the store, but it is cheap and easy to make, and you will always have fresh syrup on-hand to make cocktails. All cocktail recipes in this book are made with Simple Syrup 2:1, which is two parts of sugar and one part of water. If you prefer to use Simple Syrup 1:1, use equal parts water and sugar, but note that Simple Syrup 2:1 gives more structure to cocktails.

Usually, you will find simple syrup recipes made with hot water, but I prefer room temperature water because it gives the syrup more texture. In fact, if you boil water, it reduces the syrup, and you will not be able to control the consistency.

YIELD: 1 CUP (200 ML)

---

1 cup (200 ml) water

2 cups (400 gr) caster sugar

(1) In a jar, combine water and caster sugar, and stir until sugar is dissolved.

(2) Strain into a bottle, and store in the fridge for up to 6 months (if you make a big batch).

Bartender's Tip: Is simple syrup the same as gomme syrup? Nope. Gomme is a syrup made with the addition of gum arabica, a.k.a. the crystallized sap of the acacia tree. Gomme is thicker and gives even more texture and consistency to cocktails.

Gomme Syrup: Combine 1 cup water and ¼ cup gum Arabica powder; stir until you get a paste. In a saucepan over low heat, combine the paste with 2 cups caster sugar and stir until sugar is dissolved. Remove from heat and let it cool for 24 hours. Strain into a bottle and let it rest for another 24 hours. Store in the fridge for up to 6 months.

STRAWBERRY SYRUP

This is a sweet and tasty syrup that you can use on cakes, pancakes, ice cream, and drum roll, cocktails, such as the Berry Field (page 106)! It is so easy to make that you will not buy it anymore. And you will see the difference between yours and store-bought. A big difference. All-natural, fresh, and no artificial colors.

YIELD: 1 CUP (200 ML)

½ cup (100 grams) strawberries, washed and cut into small pieces

1 cup (200 ml) water

1 cup (200 grams) caster sugar

(1) Place cut strawberries in a saucepan and cover them with water and caster sugar.

(2) Cook over medium heat, stirring occasionally, until the sugar is dissolved (at least 20 minutes).

(3) Let it cool, then strain through a muslin cloth or fine-mesh strainer into a bottle.

(4) Store in the fridge for up to 3 weeks.

Bartender's Tip: If you would like a smoother syrup, place it in a blender and blitz until it reaches the consistency you like. If you prefer a thicker syrup, simmer longer. (Or, for a thinner syrup, simmer for less time.)

THYME-INFUSED SYRUP

This is a straightforward syrup to make, two parts sugar and one part water. It is delicious in A Naked Truth (page 74) and can be used to highlight teas and desserts too. It is a lovely herbal sweet syrup.

YIELD: 1⅔ (400 ML)

---

2 cups (400 grams) caster sugar

⅘ (200 ml) hot water

10 thyme springs, washed and dried

(1) Mix caster sugar, hot water, and thyme in a medium-sized saucepan over high heat.

(2) Cook, stirring occasionally, until sugar is dissolved.

(3) Remove from heat and let it sit for 10 minutes to cool. Strain into a bottle, cover, and store it in the fridge for up to 3 months.

TINCTURES

Bartender's Tip: You can find dropper bottles both on dedicated bar tools websites and on general houseware websites. Buy the 3 inch (50 ml) bottles because for the usage we need them, they don't need to be too big. Better to buy the glass one, too, because they are more durable and preserve better what they contain, without contaminating it.

CARDAMOM TINCTURE

A tincture is a spirit infused with spices, herbs, fruits, flowers, and vegetables. So, you can imagine how many different tinctures you can make. This one is infused with cardamom, and I chose it because in A Cloudy Mandarin (page 64), cardamom and coffee are a wonderful pairing. Tinctures enhance the flavor of a cocktail.

YIELD: 3⅓ OUNCES (100 ML)

3⅓ ounces (100 ml) mezcal

1 tablespoon (5 grams) cardamom pods

(1) In a small jar, combine mezcal and cardamom.

(2) Seal it and store it at room temperature for 1 week.

(3) Strain it into a dropper bottle. You can use cardamom tincture for up 1 month, and you can store it at room temperature.

CHILI TINCTURE

A tincture is usually made in small batches, since you just need a few drops per cocktail. If you want, you can quickly bring out the essential oils by toasting chili and spices in a dry pan before infusing. You can use any type of chili you like according to how intense you want the flavor. Try it out in a delicious Spicy Spritzo (page 114).

YIELD: 3⅓ OUNCES (100 ML)

3⅓ ounces (100 ml) over-proof spirit

2 bird's eye chilies, washed

(1) Cut chilies in half and remove any seeds.

(2) Combine chilies and over-proof spirit into a jar and seal it.

(3) Let it rest for 1 week at room temperature. Shake the jar occasionally. Strain into a bottle. Store at room temperature for up to 1 month.

SAFFRON TINCTURE

A tincture is an extraction of plant or animal material dissolved in alcohol. In this case, saffron is infused into mezcal. When you do that, saffron aromatizes mezcal and gives more intensity to the cocktails, such as Aphrodisiac Old-Fashioned (page 172). Just keep in mind that when you dissolve saffron threads, the moment they turn white, there is no more extraction, and the infusion is completed.

YIELD: 3⅓ OUNCES (100 ML)

¼ **teaspoon (0.25 gram) saffron threads**

3⅓ **ounces (100 ml) mezcal**

Combine saffron threads and mezcal in a jar, cover, and let it infuse overnight or until the threads turn white at room temperature. Store covered in the refrigerator for up to 3 weeks.

ACKNOWLEDGMENTS

Ten years ago, I would have never thought that I would find myself writing the acknowledgments of my own book one day. But here we are, and this is much a surprise for me as for anyone else. But I need to thank a few people for helping me get to this point.

First of all, I need to say thank you to my parents, Janet and Anthony. When I left Italy to start my new life ten years ago, they didn't try to stop me. They encouraged me and understood me. They always supported me and my choices, wishing me happiness and serenity.

Thank you to my friends, Marco B. and Sebastiano M., for all the time spent during our childhood. You have been an anchor, the laugh in the dark times, the hug of a brother. I thank you for the many adventures and wonderful memories that I will always carry with me.

Costantino "Costa," thank you because you are probably the first person who actually believed in me and thought I could do something good. You have been a colleague, a friend, a brother. As a colleague, you helped me learn; as a friend, you listened to my problems; and as a brother, we fought and loved each other.

Barnabas, I do not think I will be able to say thank you enough. You have been a teacher and a great help, but most of all, a friend. You taught me everything I know and even more. You introduced me to a career I did not even know I wanted. Thank you for always believing in me and for being honest with me.

Thank you, Matteo, for being one of the first people to support me and help me with this adventure. Without even knowing where my videos and pictures could go, you were ready to jump with me in any opportunities and ideas I got.

Thank you to Nana, Peter R., Rossella R., Francesco M., Roberto A., Rosita S., Jessica T., Marco B., Elena D. P., Cameron A., Anna H., Andrea A., Massimiliano N., Branca, Russ M., and Paolo S. Thanks for the support and for drinking with me. Some evenings will never be forgotten.

Thank you to my trusted tasters, Mario, Yuri, Alex and Tiziana. You never backed down and tried every drink I made, giving me honest suggestions and opinions. Thank you for helping me to create this cocktail book.

Thank you, Stefano, for realizing a project that I have wanted for a long time. Thank you for your time and help.

A special thanks to Madre Mezcal, Alipus, Cobre Negro Mezcal, Ilegal, Vago Mezcal, and Lo Verás Mezcal. Without knowing me, you trusted me and believed in my project. It was a pleasure to work with your products and create cocktails based on their flavors and characteristics.

Thank you to RG Mania, which provided me with a great selection of glassware, beautiful and elegant. They completely trusted me and had faith in me. A wonderful collaboration I will always be thankful for.

Thank you, Urban Bar. What you did for me was a grand gesture that I didn't expect. You went through a lot to deliver me an incredible selection of glassware. It was a pleasure to collaborate with you, and, hopefully, we will do so again in the future to come.

A big thank you to publisher John Whalen and Whalen Book Works, editor Margaret McGuire Novak, and designer Melissa Gerber. Without you, this book would not exist. It was a long journey, and you were there to help me at every step. You encouraged me and believed in me, and I couldn't ask for more. Thank you for your hard work and your support. The opportunity you gave me has no equal.

A special thank you to all my readers and social media supporters. Without you, surely I would never be here. Without you, I would never have opened a YouTube Channel and Instagram account. Without you, I would never be able to share the love for my job. Thank you for everything.

Last but not least, thank you, Selene, companion of my life and adventures. Since we met, you have followed me everywhere in the world and supported me in everything. Without your encouragement and words of love in times of need, all this would not have been possible. Thank you for making me a better person, both personally and professionally. To you, I dedicate all of this as a sign of a great beginning for us and our future. Tismo.

ABOUT THE AUTHOR

Emanuele Mensah is a mixologist, bar manager, photographer, and videographer based in London. He has worked for some of the best cocktail bars in the world, including Disrepute in London and Eau-de-Vie Sydney, and he was named one of the World Class Top 100 Bartenders by Diageo Reserve. On Instagram and YouTube, you can find him at Cocktails with Lele (@CocktailsWithLele), where he shows how to make excellent classic cocktails in a home bar. He teaches complex techniques as well as the basics and shares classic cocktail recipes, craft concoctions, plus innovative creations of his own.

Lele is all about sustainability and applies a zero-waste policy to his ideas and concepts; everything has a purpose and must be used. He believes in interpreting cocktails with a fresh perspective, while taking inspiration from drinks and drink recipes from the past. This means returning to the original purpose of spirits when they were used medicinally, in the mezcal of Oaxaca and around the world.

He feels that drinking a cocktail should be a moment of pleasure and sharing.

INDEX

Recipes in the book are in italics